Digging Out

How We Tunneled Our Way to Financial Independence

My Journey from Underground Miner to Real Estate Millionaire

II

Acknowledgement

I would like to thank several amazing people for helping me write this book. First of which is my amazing and beautiful wife Parham, and our children Wyatt, Caroline, and Carson who we do this for.

To my family who have all stuck with me through this journey and who have supported me throughout the entire journey thank you! Special thanks to Mom and Dad for all the help and guidance along the way. My wife Parham for going along with my crazy ideas and always being there helping and doing the essential things to make this dream of ours work.

Stephanie Hyde did an awesome job editing this book. If you notice the fact that there are paragraphs and chapters that is all her work. I simply gave her 55,000 words strung together and she suffered through the arduous process of making my random thoughts into something comprehensible.

I would also like to thank Gary Pallini, well actually his wonderful wife and daughters for, allowing him the time and opportunity to truly make a difference in people's lives with his teaching and mentorship. Gary has been instrumental in helping people like me discover the benefits of financial freedom through real estate investing.

Linda Baltzell for being the only person to ever take me seriously when I talked of my goal of retiring by age 40. Linda, you believed in me and we did it, thank you! It really is the little things in life that people do that make all the difference.

Finally, I would like to thank Pete Livingston, Terry Morrow, and Bill Dunn for showing me how to treat people right and run a business with integrity.

Table of Contents

Digging Out

How We Tunneled Our Way to Financial Independence

Digging Out is the story of my personal journey to financial independence. It begins with my entry into the "real world," and goes on to describe my experience of joining the corporate world, discovering the endless cycle of the "Rat Race," and finally details my exit to the world of financial independence through real estate investing. My goal is to keep you, the reader, entertained and excited about what all is possible through this alternative means of earning a living. Throughout this book, I will offer bits of advice on how to excel in the simple yet complicated world of real estate investing and share some of the many mistakes that I made along the way.

It is my hope that you, the reader and real estate investor, take the time to truly think over the advice that is sprinkled throughout the story that I am about to share with you. It has cost me tens of thousands of dollars to attend the School of Hard Knocks, and this book may very well be a partial scholarship and fast track towards graduation for those who pay attention.

As I wrote this book, I was struck by just how meticulously "the system" (our standard education and typical list of options) is designed to paint us all into a box of becoming one thing: an employee. To become financially independent, you need to act and think in ways that are different from what you've been taught your whole life. My path out of "the system" was real estate, whatever you choose as your path, please remember that you must start thinking and acting outside of what you consider normal in order to live a life that is anything but normal.

Chapter 1: You Can Do It

If I can make it in this business, then you surely can. The only place where I have truly excelled is in my complete unwillingness to give up. I managed to graduate in the top 25% of my high school class, and was one of seven from that same group to go to Virginia Tech for engineering. Of those seven, I am the only one to have graduated with an engineering degree. Most of those other guys and gals were smarter than me, but when challenged they just moved on to something better suited for them. You will find the same is true in real estate investing: once people figure out there is a lot of work involved, they move on to something else. I stuck with engineering and passed calculus with a B- on my fifth attempt, long after my friends had all thrown in the towel. To the complete dismay of my many professors at Virginia Tech, I continued on in engineering despite their advice. Finally, after five long years I graduated last in my class of 5000 people. I was officially an engineer! I made it! Since that day, no one has ever asked me for my GPA or how many times I took calculus. The truth is, no one cares, all they care about is that I graduated. Once in the real world grades no longer matter, results matter.

My approach to real estate investing was much like my approach to engineering; my first several properties didn't go very well but I kept at it. Today, I can honestly say that I'm proud to be a full-fledged professional real estate investor and School of Hard Knocks Doctoral Student. It doesn't matter what I paid in tuition, or how many times I took Land Lording 101, it was all worth it. Needless to say, the tools necessary for me to be successful were learned at the School of Hard Knocks and I call upon those tools regularly to avoid receiving additional "remedial coursework."

I have done well in real estate, and you can too. You don't need to be a genius to make it in this business, but you do need sheer determination. In the mines we called it "stick-to-it-iveness," and while most people don't have it, those who do, do well. Those of us who succeed at investing are the ones that put in the long hours and stick with it through the good times and bad. In the end, it all comes down to buying the right property at the right price and then executing your exit or hold strategy. You will make mistakes, as we all have. Learn from them and move on.

Prior to starting our real estate investing careers, most of us investors have had another more mundane career. In most cases, the careers we went to school for weren't fulfilling us the way we'd hoped, and for that reason we began to seek an alternative path.

As you are now reading this book, reality has probably set in and you have realized that you are stuck in the Rat Race as just another cog in the system. You probably fell for the same thing that us professional investors fell for: an awe-inspiring story about how if we just go to college and get good grades, we will get everything we ever dreamt of. While this may be true in a small amount of cases, most of us simply go out into the world and have careers that only represent a paycheck to us. My career was a little less mundane than most, but in the end, I was just another person competing in the Rat Race and working my tail off to help make other people rich. The only difference between you and the professional investor is that the professional investor got sick and tired of the Rat Race and found a path out.

Finding a path out is something that I encourage everyone to consider. At the very worst, you may find that this isn't a path for you, and you can move on. At the very best, however, you may discover your path to financial freedom and the bliss it can bring.

Chapter 2: My First Job

My career started in the mines. Working in the mines can be a fun profession as every day is a new adventure. You actually get paid to blow things up! Us underground miners are a very close-knit community; you count on each other every day to keep yourself safe. We all want to make it out alive, and to do so you better be able to trust the guy beside you.

Most likely the guy beside you is fairly rough around the edges, with a "work hard play hard" mentality. He's also most likely very poorly educated and a little slow on the uptake. The following is my story from working full-time in the mines to working full-time for myself in real estate.

My path into and out of the rat race started innocently enough in one of the largest open pit mines on earth: Phelps Dodge Morenci in Morenci, Arizona (currently Freeport McMoRan Copper and Gold). This was my first job out of college, and I was excited to be earning my own way. Morenci was, and still is, a company town in the middle of nowhere. 99% of people in Arizona can't find Morenci on a map, and the 1% who can stay the hell away. Morenci literally is a company town. I lived in a company house, drove a company truck and shopped at the company store. I know what you're thinking, and no, I did not work there in the 1950's. I started in 2004, and while it may be difficult to believe, company towns still existed in remote parts of the country at that time.

I started at Morenci as a junior mining engineer and was privileged to live in a 3-bedroom company ~~house~~ shanty. When I moved in there were no appliances, no working toilets, no air conditioning and the floors were bare concrete. My shanty had recently been painted and the scorpions that infested the place were literally entombed on the walls as the company painters had

3

sprayed right over them. I didn't know exactly what I had gotten myself into at that point, but I was going to figure it out real quick. My initiation into the real world was going to be complete culture shock.

Several recent college graduates were hired at the same time as me, and we all lived on the same block. My next-door neighbor, Sam, and I worked out a deal where we'd each use our $2,000 sign-on bonuses to furnish our houses, co-op style. Let's be honest, $2,000 doesn't go very far, but $4,000? Now that's something. Sam got to the store first and bought us a refrigerator, stove and a big screen TV. I made the two and a half hour journey to the closest town with a Home Depot the following weekend and got us a grill, microwave, dishwasher and window unit air conditioner. For the next several months, Sam and I would hang out and get dinner. If it was at my place, dinner was either burgers or brats as I only owned a grill to cook with. Sam was able to get a little more creative since he owned a stove, spaghetti was his main stay. Needless to say, there was a lot of eating out at one of the four restaurants in the thriving metropolis of Morenci. You had your choice of the Kopper Kettle Kafe (abbreviated as KKK), or you could consider the pizza place, the bowling alley, or last but not least the Dairy Queen. No small southwestern town is complete without a DQ, and our DQ was undoubtably the best restaurant within 50 miles.

Living in a remote mining camp really made me question some of the choices that I had made in life. There were quite a few times that first year that I thought, "WOW, I spent five years in college to end up here!?" Maybe I should have drank a few less beers and only spent four years in college." I guess some of us just have to learn the hard way. Life was generally good though, there was a consistent paycheck, and as a single guy living in a company house, I virtually had no bills. My rent was $174 per month, and

4

both water and electric were provided by the mine at next to nothing. The last increase in water or electric rates had been in 1983, over twenty years earlier. In general, I was living pretty high on the hog. Truth be told, I had too much money. There is only so much bowling that you can do, and the company knew that.

At the mines, we were expected to work a minimum of 50 hour weeks. My boss was an overachiever and liked to schedule me for 12 hour days, plus one weekend a month. This left me very little time for spending my money (not that I had a whole lot of places or things to spend my money on in the middle of nowhere during the "Amazon.com-less," dark ages). To help with this problem, I decided to invest in my 401(K). I decided to put 30% of my salary into retirement savings. Man, was it exciting to watch my retirement savings grow, especially when it was growing quickly. This 401(K) money would later come in handy as it purchased two houses and got me out of PMI on my first house.

My job at the mine was to determine where we shipped the ore that we mined. I had to designate it as high grade to be sent for special processing, regular grade to be sent to leach piles or waste. This was a phenomenally boring job. I almost never made it out of my cubical, which I had to share with another person. Yeah, I know what you are thinking; I must have been pretty low on the totem pole to be at the point where I had to share a cubicle. Frankly, my place on the totem pole was the part that was buried underground.

I shared a cubicle with Monica, Monica was nice but we had zero privacy and during our time together I learned way too much about her personal life (and she mine). We sat back to back, and with our shared space being so small, I literally had to tell her when I was getting up so she could scoot her chair in and I could squeeze out. Neither of us could push our chairs back to stand up

5

without telling the other first. Needless to say, I knew every time she sneezed, farted or had to pee.

Worse yet was the job. The computers that we had were state of the art but the program that we were running on them was so poorly written that it took about an hour each morning for the computers to load. As the low man on the totem pole, I had the enviable task of showing up an hour early each day to start the process of running the computer program. I had to babysit the computers the whole time as the program would stop and ask you to hit "enter" at several random times throughout the start-up process. If you went to the bathroom, got a cup of coffee or just went to stretch your legs, you would often come back to the screen asking you to press "enter" to continue. Murphy's Law taught me to just stay put every morning so that the loading process would go uninterrupted. You can only imagine the "feeling of fulfillment" I got from spending the first hour of the workday staring at four blank screens just waiting for the random "press enter to continue" message to appear.

If I didn't have the computers up and running when everyone got in, things went from bad to worse. Everyone would go get coffee and stand around and bullshit while I was stuck there staring at those infuriating screens. An absolute moron could have done this part of the job, which made sense because we were more or less treated like absolute morons. Unfortunately, I had come to feel like quite the moron myself in putting up with this morning routine.

As if the whole monotonous process of showing up before everyone else was not bad enough, the day only got worse from there. At about 11:00 am, my morning duties were pretty much finished. Once I had completed all of my daily reports and uploaded all of the new data into the computers, I was left in a holding pattern until 1:00pm when the lab would have the assay

6

results back from ore mined during the night. I could not sign off for the day until I had received and posted the new data from the lab.

Again, I was left feeling like a moron sitting there wasting my life away with nothing to do for two hours, knowing that at 1:00 I would receive about four to five hours' worth of work. Hurry up and wait was the game, and I have never played that game well. Once the lab results finally came in, I would work feverishly to try and get everything done as fast as possible so my 11 hour work day could come to an end. You can only imagine how maddening it is to watch everyone in the office leave at 3:00 p.m., knowing all too well that your day both starts earlier and ends later than theirs' does. Yep, I had the worst job at the mine, and I knew it.

My desire to exit the Rat Race started almost instantly, it just took me a while to find my exit path. When I finally left this job my boss told me how the company had really struggled to keep engineers in this position, they all kept quitting, and he could not understand why. He was serious, he just could not understand why people didn't like that job. I was stunned, I just replied that maybe the job wasn't for everyone… he should read this book.

Chapter 3: Learning You Can't Win

One day my boss, Joe, called me into his office and gave me a complete ass chewing regarding the "quality of my work". He told me he had spent the entire weekend, "over 16 hours in the office fixing mistakes that I had made". He went on to lament that he had only gotten a portion of my mistakes fixed, and that I would have to do the rest on my own time. Completely flabbergasted, I didn't have a clue what he was talking about. I was sure that I had been doing a good job, as I always followed the manual step by step. I tried my best to explain this to Joe, but his only response was to open his computer and begin running the program so he could proceed to point out all the errors he felt I had made.

Once the program had loaded, he about fell out of his chair. All of the errors he had spent the weekend fixing were back! Joe was one pissed off boss-man. Turns out he had failed to save the file in the correct location, and it had been automatically overwritten when I came in that morning and loaded the program. Perhaps Joe should have showed up to work a little earlier that day, or at least known how the program worked. This would not be the first or last time that Joe would be a major source of frustration for his staff. Unfortunately, and due to no fault of his own, he had been thrown into a job that he didn't truly understand, and it left him woefully out of touch with the realities of his subordinates' daily struggles.

Once Joe got over the shock of learning that 16 hours of work were gone, he explained to me that I was creating what he referred to as, "triple point errors". He didn't know that our training book specifically instructed us to ignore these warnings, as they were unavoidable. I tried to explain to him that they were warnings, not errors, because the program had continued to run and wouldn't be able to do so if it was compiling errors. Warnings, on the other hand, were simply the software's way of telling us something could be wrong, and we may want to investigate further. The warnings were due to a bug in one of the functions that we were using that most companies didn't use. We couldn't run the software without generating these warnings. I pointed out that there were something like 40,000 warnings being shown as of the time I had started in the role only a few months earlier. Joe fired back with the comment that there were no warnings in Monica's work. Talk about frustrating, Monica was the golden child and could do no wrong. I never did tell Joe that Monica had simply turned off the warning feature. I couldn't betray my cube mate like that. No worries though, I would turn that feature off going forward and my work would look perfect too. It was days like that that further illuminated just how badly I needed a different way, a better way, to earn a living.

About 8 months into my job, Joe called me into his office again. When I got there Joe was at his desk and Jim was standing around. Apparently, they were waiting on me to begin. The meeting went quickly. Jim and I were informed that the company had hired some interns. Our department would be receiving a female intern, and as the lone males under 50 in the group we were explicitly informed to avoid fraternizing with the intern.

Now, I am not the smartest person on earth, but I got the distinct feeling that Jim was not there to receive this lecture so much as to serve as a witness. Jim was one of Joe's only friends in the group and while he was under 50 it was only by a few months, and he had just celebrated his 24th wedding anniversary. I on the other hand was 22 and single... Not only was this conversation offensive, it was very much par for the course. "We are going to own you every minute of every day, and we will even dictate what you do in your spare time in *our* town."

Regardless, avoiding the intern shouldn't have been hard, as Joe had me working 60+ hour weeks and, due to attrition, I was now working every other weekend instead of one weekend per month.

Chapter 4: Life Happens

Sometimes things that shouldn't be difficult are simply that. My neighbor, Sam, had the hots for one of the interns in his department, and he had conveniently arranged for me to host a welcome party for all the interns at my place. He was even so kind as to notify all of the female interns himself. This "staying away from the interns" business was not off to a good start. The night of the party, I had my shanty all cleaned up, and we moved Sam's table and chairs over to my place (because I only had a picnic table by the grill). As a typical single guy just out of college, a table and/or chairs were still pretty low on my priority list. Besides, it wasn't like I was getting a lot of visitors. We filled the fridge with booze and bought some brats to grill.

The party that night went well. Sam had a swing and a miss with the intern he had the hots for, but he had not struck out completely. They became good friends and spent a lot of time together that summer. Meanwhile, I noticed that the intern working in my department was something special and we ended up going on our first date the following weekend.

Now I had to figure out how to keep my boss out of the loop in a painfully small town where everyone knows everyone. Luckily, no one liked my boss and he didn't pick up on too much gossip. No one suspected a thing until I got dreadfully sick with some inexplicable ailment and, after taking a week off, it was our intern who curiously volunteered to make the two and a half hour drive with me to the nearest doctor in Tucson. Though we'd been discrete up until then, the whispers had started and the cat was out of the bag.

This actually made life a lot simpler, now all I had to do was focus on my boss not finding out. Lia, the intern's boss, was completely in on Project Cover Up. She understood the situation well as she had ended up marrying one of her employees (which eventually resulted in his termination from the company). Thanks to Lia's assistance running interference and scheduling triage, Parham (that's the intern's name, by the way) and I enjoyed many three-day adventures that summer. We managed to go the whole summer without my boss ever figuring anything out. At last, the summer was over and Parham went back to finishing her Master's Degree at beautiful Fort Collins, Colorado. Meanwhile, I was stuck in the job from hell in a county that had a whopping three nationally franchised businesses: a Circle K gas station, a company-ran Chevron gas station and the best restaurant in 50 miles, the Dairy Queen.

Immediately after Parham went back to Colorado, I managed to contract yet another inexplicable illness. I was very fortunate that my sister had flown in from Virginia to visit. She went with me to the company doctor and didn't like his bedside manner or the fact that he refused to consider any other treatment options beyond the one he'd recommended. He told my sister flat out that, "if this doesn't cure him, I will pay for the burial." Little did that crappy company doc know he almost had to put his money where his mouth was.

My sister and her husband were four hours away at my grandmother's house when they decided that I really should see a different doctor. They immediately drove back to Morenci, put me in a car and we made the four hour drive back to the hospital near my grandmother's house.

In the meantime, my 85-year-old grandmother, who was afraid of doctors, went to the hospital and checked herself in to the emergency room just so she could talk to a doctor about what the doctor in Morenci had diagnosed me with. The doctor, while annoyed that a perfectly healthy person was in the emergency room, was very kind and told her that I should immediately be taken to a major medical center if my diagnosis was correct, as they couldn't treat me at their facility.

Back to my four hour ride to the hospital, I was really starting to get in bad shape. When we finally arrived at the hospital, I was entering septic shock. The emergency room nurse took one look at my leg where my skin was turning black and had me placed into quarantine. It is a little unnerving when a nurse puts you into a room and you hear the deadbolt locking from the outside. The doctor/surgeon showed up in less than five minutes and off they went removing a section of my thigh. This doctor seemed to know what he was doing and praised my sister quite a bit for getting me the care I needed.

I was assured that I would have lost my leg if she had not gotten me to the hospital when she did. I ended up spending the next two weeks in the hospital. Both my parents and my new girlfriend flew in to make sure I was alright. I am glad I wasn't there for that awkward introduction. My mom picked Parham up from the airport, and they all stayed at the same place (Grandma's house) for the next two weeks. I guess that is when I really knew that this intern was in it for the long haul. Parham and the folks got along well. It seems like the women in my life are somehow always there when I'm in need. I don't know if they are the cure or cause of my problems, but either way I consider myself fortunate. They always get me through when things are tough.

Everyone was happy with my recovery but me. Two weeks was a nice paid vacation from the mine, but I really could have used more. My break was just long enough to get me thinking about what direction I wanted to go in life. I knew this: I hated my job babysitting computers and I was beginning to realize that unless I changed something, I would be working there for the next 30 years trying to make someone else rich.

13

Not only was the job really starting to wear on me, but so was the prospect of never realizing my ambitions. I needed a better job, the pay at the bottom stinks and the only thing worse are the hours. I could no longer justify trading every other weekend and 60 hours per week of my life for just enough money to get by on. Yes, I was saving a good bit of my paycheck, 30% going into my 401(k), but you can't touch that money until you are 59 ½ years old. So there I was, 23 years old, living on $2,026 monthly take home pay, 1-2 hours away from any from of civilization, and no end in sight. I could only dream about how great retirement would be…in 36 ½ years. Something needed to change, and whatever that was was completely up to me.

Chapter 5: Supervising at the Old Hickory Mine

I don't know how people justify giving their best years away to someone else for a salary that's just enough to get by on. I just couldn't do it anymore. I decided to quit my job and find something that made me happy and allowed me to enjoy life. Parham and I moved in together in Colorado where she was finishing up her master's degree. While there, I looked for a job that would not cost me the best years of my life. Parham had a single requirement, and that was that the next job had to be in a location that was within half an hour of civilization. We defined civilization as a town big enough to have both a Walmart and a Target.

After about two months in Colorado, I accepted a position as a supervisor at a small titanium sand operation in rural Stony Creek, Virginia. It was there that I learned what hard work really was. I was one of four supervisors in the rotation at the Old Hickory Mine. We were working supervisors, which means that we spent time down in the trenches with the men turning the wrenches. Life at the mine was tough, we worked 12 hour shifts that required constant physical labor.

Our mill was a reproduction of another mill currently running in the Australian desert. In Australia, the mills had no exterior siding and no roofs. This may have worked well in the desert, but not so well in Virginia where it rains and snows. Our mill ended up getting upgraded with siding and a roof, this however created a new problem. In Australia, every mill had a crane that would simply lift supplies up to the top floor of the building whenever they were needed (most of our equipment was located on the top floor). The crane system worked very well in Australia, too bad we now had a non-removable roof on our mill.

So, here in the good ol' U.S. of A., we had the luxury of carrying all of our supplies up and down five sets of stairs every time they were needed. Have a major breakdown? Need to replace screens on the top floor? No problem, the screens only weighed about 75 lbs and carrying them up five flights of steps saved me a gym membership. As a supervisor it was my job to set the pace for the crew. It was physically demanding work, but I did my job well.

I learned a lot about hard work and it's benefits during my time in Virginia. The crews and supervisors who didn't work as hard didn't make the production that we made. Eventually, when things went south, the low producers were the first to lose their jobs. Today, as a professional investor, I watch those that truly work hard achieve unimaginable success, while those that think this is a get rich quick business go broke fast.

As a mill supervisor, I received three weeks of training prior to being given my own crew. My crew was comprised entirely of misfits and castoffs. On my very first day leading a crew, I asked one of my employees to help me carry some of those screens up to the fifth floor. He argued with me that nothing up there was broken, and he didn't feel we needed to get them up there at this time. I told him that when the screens did fail, I would like to be ready with the parts staged to fix them (screens failed at least once every rotation). At the end of the shift this employee said to me, "I am not going to work for an asshole like you," and promptly quit. I would later learn that he was going to be fired the next day for falsifying documents. They always say first days are the hardest, right?

I had a rough crew to say the least. If I wanted to climb the corporate ladder, and eventually become rich and retire early, I needed to get these bums to be top producers. At this point, I had decided that I would get out of the Rat Race through advancement. Note to reader: advancement is not the best route out, but I had to find that out on my own. One misfit down, two to go. Next up was Bobby, this kid was rough. He didn't have the brains God gave a fruit fly. When there was work was to be done, he was always missing. When he was around, all you wanted was for him to be missing.

Once we had the front-end loader get stuck in the mud. I asked Bobby and Mark (aka Bat Boy, more on the source of the nickname later) to go and get it unstuck. Bobby wanted to use the bulldozer to get it out. Who was I to argue? I had only been there a few months and Bobby had been around for a couple of years. I was pretty confident that using the bulldozer for our issue was a little bit of overkill, but hell it would get the job done.

About two hours later, I received a radio call from Bobby and Mark that they needed my assistance. "My truck is stuck, and I need to get it out!" Bobby yelled at me over the radio.

"What the hell are you doing in your truck?" I asked.

Bobby replied, "I am doing exactly what you told me to do!"

Confused, I responded, "what do you think I told you to do?"

"You told me to get the front-end loader out of the mud" Bobby replied.

Still confused, I decided that I should go see what the problem was. I left the mill and headed to the mining area. When I got there, I found Bobby and his personal pickup truck buried to the axels in the mud. There was a chain going from the back bumper of his truck to the bulldozer. Yes, these two guys thought that their 1987 Dodge 4X4 with oversized tires and a lift kit could pull an 80,000lb bulldozer out of the mud. Meanwhile, the bulldozer was still chained to the front-end loader.

17

Apparently, Bobby had gotten the bulldozer stuck while trying to get the front-end loader unstuck. According to Bobby, Mark had forgotten to release the brakes on the front-end loader when they tried to pull it out and now both machines were buried in the mud. By the time Bobby had turned to his truck for a solution, there was no other equipment available and the wonder boy figured his, "4-wheel drive Dodge with oversized tires and lift kit could do the trick." It was then and there that I realized the error in my ways. I didn't give Bobby or Mark much credit in the IQ department, but my God they had even less common sense than I could have possibly imagined. I would not make this mistake again.

Exasperated I told the two of them to get into my truck and we headed back to the mill. This was going to be one for the dayshift guys. Bobby could get a ride home with Mark once this shift was over.

Shift change couldn't get here soon enough. Transitions between shifts usually occurred in the meeting room over a cup of hot coffee, but not today. I met Rob, the oncoming supervisor, in the parking lot.

"What you got?" Rob asked in his southern drawl.

"A problem" I replied.

I didn't know what to do with my group of misfits, but this was getting ridiculous. After recounting the events to Rob, he insisted that I go with him to show him the situation myself. We had a great laugh, and Rob assured me that he would get the equipment out on dayshift.

Rob, as always, was true to his word. The following night I showed up early and there was Bobby's truck, sitting in the very first parking spot. It was missing the rear bumper, but other than that the truck didn't appear to have any damage. The same could not be said for Bobby's pride, or his bumper which would remain chained to the bulldozer to be drug around for the following month. Dayshift was quite pleased with their little trophy, and they made sure that Bobby knew it.

Though I would later find that I would do everything in my power to avoid staying in the field my degree had prepared me for, at this moment I was focused on finding a better crew so I could make it in the mining business. After things had settled down a little bit and the bumper incident was a thing of the past, Bobby made my crew a little better for me. It was yet another shift where work needed to be done and Bobby was nowhere to be found. By this time, the only remaining misfits were Bobby and Mark. The new guys were getting tired of performing all of the work, while the senior guys always found somewhere else to be just before things went south. Today, they decided they were going to set Bobby up.

With a little bit of help from a contractor, the new guys made our mining machine break down while Bobby was at it performing busy work. The breakdown meant that Bobby had to go inside the mixing tank and clear out debris. The mixing tank was filled waist high with a mixture of sand, clay and 35 degree water. The only way to remove the debris from the tank was to feel around for it with your feet. Once you found the offending item that wouldn't pass through the screens on the bottom of the tank, it had to be pulled out. I never found a way to pull out the debris without getting fully submerged in freezing cold muddy water. Apparently, Bobbyy didn't have a miracle solution either. There are few things worse than stripping down to your skivvies and jumping in freezing cold water for $13.50 an hour. For Bobby, who was now heading back to the mill for a quick rinse off and a new pair of underwear, things were about to get worse.

Another call came over the radio for debris in the sump. Bobby went back to the mining area to perform this miserable job yet again, and on his way back he proceeded to let his displeasure of getting the short straw (aka actually doing his job) be known. Unfortunately for Bobby, his venting did not fall on deaf ears. He broadcasted his feelings over the radio and too many people heard his tirade for it to be ignored. Two down.

In mining, most everyone earns a nickname at some point in time. Usually these nicknames are not very flattering, but almost always very telling. Mark, my last remaining misfit, earned his nick name the hard way. He had forever become "Bat Boy". When we were on days off, Mark took his new girlfriend to a party about a mile down the road from where he lived with his wife. Unfortunately, Mark was completely unaware that this party happened to be at his wife's cousin's farmhouse. Mark's marriage may have worked out better if he had spent more time interacting with his wife and her family and less time out partying with other women.

After Mark showed up with his new girlfriend, he promptly realized that he had made a mistake and tried to talk his way out of this predicament with the cousin. The cousin was not having any of it and proceeded to call Mark's wife and inform her of the girlfriend situation. Now it was time for Mark to make a quick exit, however his getaway was stalled by an upset girlfriend who just found out that her boyfriend was married. This gave Mark's wife just enough time to make it to the party before he was able to leave. With his escape plan shot, he tried to calm his wife down. She had shown up with a baseball bat, and when he admitted to having a girlfriend she made him pay. She must have been pretty mad because she didn't stop when she broke his ribs, or when she broke his leg, nor did she stop when she broke his back. Her cousin, not wanting her to go to jail for murder, finally stepped in and saved poor Mark's life.

Mark did eventually recover from the beating. He ended up missing just under three months of work and walked from then on with a permanent limp. Upon his return to work at the mines, he was forever known as Bat Boy. With Bat Boy as my only misfit left, things were starting to look up.

Working at a mine is a little different than your normal 9 to 5 but not so much so. Sure, we had some obstacles to overcome like the time that our mining machine froze to the ground. I was working nights when that catastrophe happened. I showed up to start my first night shift of our rotation and was told by Rob that we had been screwed. The outgoing shift, led by Bolo (who was now enjoying four days off), had left the water running and the mining machine with a major leak. In the freezing temperatures, the mining machine had frozen to the ground. Rob's guys had worked most of the day gathering the pickaxes and blow torches that we would need to chip away the frozen mud around the machine.

Tools at the ready, it would be my crew that was tasked with actually doing the work. It was a miserable 15 degrees outside, and it took us every bit of 12 hours chipping ice to get the machine ready to be moved. We had been on a good run, and the lost production from that missed shift knocked us out of the number 1 position for the month. Worse yet, it put Bolo's crew in first place. We really did get screwed. We went home the next morning cold, exhausted and in second place for the production bonus. Meanwhile Rob's crew got the machine free within an hour of the start of their shift and got all the credit for fixing the situation.

See, mining is just like any other office job: you do the work, the other guy gets all the credit, and the jackass that caused the whole problem walks away without ever knowing he did anything wrong. Worse yet, that same jackass ends up with the "performer of the month" award.

All that being said, I really did enjoy my time supervising at the mine. The good thing about shift work is the time off. We worked four days on and four days off. Parham, now my fiancé, and I got to spend a lot of time together and do all sorts of great things on those four day weekends. We traveled quite a bit, went camping and spent quite a bit of time (and money) working on our fixer upper of a home. Life was great, and those are some of my fondest memories. However, it was obvious that while my work life balance was greatly improved, my chances of retiring early were non-existent.

Chapter 6: Moving Up

I had been saving a fortune in my 401(K), which was disappearing just as fast as I was putting money into it. It was now 2007, and the economy was crashing. My savings were disappearing and at this rate, even with the level of savings that I'd been stockpiling, retirement was going to be sometime after 59 ½. I needed to find a better way. I was beginning to realize that the Rat Race was just that. I was a slave to someone else's dreams and goals, and I would never be free until I could provide for my family on my own. I realized that my job was holding me back from achieving my dreams and living as I saw fit. I just didn't know how to leave the stability and paycheck from my job and still survive.

I chose the safe path forward which included accepting a promotion into the engineering department to oversee projects and support operational groups as needed. This new job was a step up in pay and while the hours weren't great, they weren't bad either. Though I was happy to be promoted, it dawned on me that I had just traded a little more of my time for a little more money (I bet my hourly wage didn't change at all!). The added tradeoff was increased accountability, no longer could I simply hang up my jacket and leave when the day was over. As a manager, everything was on my plate.

My new management position required me to work late if I had a major project going on, or perhaps even work on weekends to ensure projects ran smoothly and that everyone had what they needed when they showed up to work on Monday. All this extra responsibility for just under $200 per month take home pay. This promotion was really starting to feel like a poor trade.

Furthermore, as part of the management group I was now officially part of the leadership team and that means stepping up to help out when needed. Parham and I had plans to go out of town and visit her family on Thanksgiving weekend. It was one of the few chances that we had to visit relatives as I had only two weeks per year of vacation time. This long weekend was going to be nice, until something went wrong at work.

We had a contractor get upset that there wasn't enough work prepared for his crew to stay busy over the long weekend. Both my boss and I insisted that there was plenty of work laid out for his guys and that he should not be concerned. The contractor wouldn't hear any of that, which meant that I would need to work well into the night on Wednesday evening to plan more work for them. I ended up being the very last salaried employee to leave the facility that night by several hours. This effectively canceled day one of our vacation, forcing us to leave on Thanksgiving Day and battle the heavily congested drive through the Washington DC area.

Upon returning to work on Monday, I was met with a major headache. None of the extra work that I had stayed late for had been completed. In fact, the majority of the work that we had originally laid out for the contractor was not completed! No apologies came from the contractor, nor did they acknowledge that they had made a mistake. Better yet, I never even received so much as a thank you or kind word from my boss for the extra effort that I had put in. Once again, I had traded valuable family time for work. This time it just stung more because the work had been completely pointless. It would be another two weeks before the contractor was able to finish the work that I had laid out for them.

This was the first of many times in my career that I would learn about how not to lead people. We had allowed our contractor, who worked for us, to determine how and when they would work and be paid. Furthermore, we allowed them to tell us what to do and essentially proved to them that we were their employees, it was not the other way around. If they didn't like what a project manager had to say, they just had to go above their head and they could get whatever they wanted. I later found out that our site manager had a weekly tee time with our primary contractor. So, the real problem was that the guy at the top didn't want to piss off his golfing buddy.

Parts of me truly enjoyed this new role despite the occasional headaches, but I couldn't shake the feeling that there was something missing. I felt like I was stuck on that predetermined path of retiring at 65. I didn't see much of a way to get around that inevitability. As I struggled with this dilemma, things back at my fixer upper of a home were getting better. We had nearly completed our renovations and I had become pretty handy along the way.

Chapter 7: Our First Home

In 2005, shortly after I'd started working in Virginia, we purchased our first house and it was a true fixer upper. I purchased this house without Parham getting to see it first. I figured, why not? It's in my name and I am buying it with my money. Well, let me tell you why not. Apparently, she could get upset about pretty much everything. I have mostly blocked those conversations from memory, but they went something like this: "we are supposed to make decisions together, I haven't even seen a picture… you spent how much?" Then, after the pictures were sent to her (we didn't have cell phone cameras back then you know) it moved on to: "I don't like the color, why is there a fire hydrant in the back yard? What is that weird door for?" Twelve years later, I am still suffering from that decision. My wife reminds me of it every month when the rent comes in (or doesn't) and at tax time when we write off yet another year of loss. But hey, my mother loved the house.

Our new home was a real winner, nearly condemned and complete with a Darwin door. (For those of you who don't know what a Darwin door is, it's a second story exterior door that opens out onto the deck. Except in our case, the deck was missing). The deck appeared to have collapsed years earlier and now the door simply led to a two-story drop. Thus, the name Darwin door. A few months into the journey of home ownership, our insurance company would have a field day with this. They notified us that they were canceling our policy unless the door situation was resolved in 30 days. They also complained that the house didn't look like it was being lived in… We were living in it, it was just a real fixer upper and looked rough.

Our house was also equipped with a huge four car garage, all it was missing was the garage door and roof. However, since it sat ninety degrees from the street you couldn't even tell the flat roof and garage door were missing until you got pretty close. However, in getting that close you'd also notice that there were a couple of drums of used motor oil stored back there too. Most of the drums were full, but a few had managed to leak out all over the ground (side note: to the folks at Carquest, I still owe you for helping to dispose of all that, thank you!). Amazingly, with all of the toxic sludge and contamination on the ground, there was no adverse impact on the growth of vegetation. If anything, Mother Nature had proven her strength (and lack of sense of humor) in growing unwieldy thorn bushes near where the used motor oil had been.

The only other remarkable exterior feature of the house was the missing siding above the master bedroom window. This hole in the siding gave small animals access into the attic. Mostly pigeons it would seem, judging by the massive amounts of bird poop in the attic.

Once inside, the house actually wasn't that bad if you could see passed the paint job. Both of the downstairs bathrooms were fully functional, the original hardwood floors were beautiful and the insulation-free plaster walls had all been sheet rocked over, giving a nice touch of modernization. It was generally livable.

Upstairs, the master bedroom was perfect except for the unfinished closet and strange dip in the floor near the addition. I had to ask; how does a master bedroom closet remain unfinished for 90 years? I would come to find out that many generations of lazy people had owned this house, but hey I was going to make a fortune on this property one day. This was my American Dream. The master bathroom was completely unusable, and the other two bedrooms were interesting to say the least. The second bedroom had a new window added to it, by the creative use of a Sawzall and a storm window. Yep, that storm window was all that kept the cold air inside from meeting up with the colder air outside in the winter months. The third bedroom was an addition off of the second bedroom, and someone had thought it would be a good idea to attach a sunroom to this second story bedroom. It must have been pretty awkward to get to the sunroom in the morning by having to walk through both the second and third bedrooms. That is the only way that I can explain the Darwin door leading out of the sunroom. All that being said, I was convinced that this house would be great once fixed up!

Heck, I knew a deal when I saw one and this was the house for me. At only $93,000, this jalopy was a steal. Back in '05, the housing bubble was growing rapidly and no other house on the street had sold for less than $100K. I was going to make a fortune on this puppy. Just a little bit of sweat equity and we would be on our way.

My handyman skills grew considerably during those first couple of years. First, I learned how to replace windows. This skill arose from sheer necessity. Let's just say that fixing the hole in our siding would lead me to serving my first eviction notice (even if it was just to a family of pigeons). But pigeons are clever, fixing the siding only encouraged them to move onto the roof directly above the repaired hole and they let it be known that they would NOT be leaving. Those darn pigeons sat there all summer and into fall, crapping on our front stoop. Lesson learned: done the wrong way, evictions can create a whole new set of problems, sometimes well into the future.

What do pigeons have to do with learning to replace windows you ask? Well, turns out I actually have very bad aim. One morning I threw a rock at the pigeons and while I missed the intended pigeon by about ten feet, I had no problem hitting our master bedroom window. Immediately, just like a Charlie Brown cartoon, a circle of glass just fell out of the window. I have never seen a window break like before. It didn't shatter, it didn't crack, just a 12-inch circular piece of glass came loose and fell on the floor of our master bedroom. Somehow, that circular piece didn't break when it hit the floor. How in the heck does a ¼ inch rock make a 12 inch diameter hole in a window? I cussed at the pigeons one more time as I taped the piece of glass back into the window and headed to Lowe's. This was the first of 18 windows that we would end up replacing in that house.

Chapter 8: Being in Charge

January 2007 started with another promotion, I was now Superintendent of the Concord Mine (sister mine to the Old Hickory Mine). This was a pretty major role, especially for someone of my age. I was excited to be in charge of my own department and knew that success or failure depended on me. I eagerly traded more of my time for a couple more dollars in my pocket. In fact, the promotion brought with it so little money that I had to stop and ask my boss what was going on with the salary because it just wasn't competitive. My boss informed me that his superiors believed that he had taken a real risk putting a 25-year-old in charge of a multimillion dollar operation. Apparently, not everyone at the top was convinced that this was a great idea, or that I had the ability to succeed. He believed in me but stated that the salary would come when I proved I could handle the role.

Well, I was going to prove that I deserved a salary similar to everyone else at my tier in the company. With my acceptance of the new position came a $500 per year raise, and I was now fully committed to being on the career employee track. I was hooked, I fell for the great scam that title and responsibility equate to success. All of my family and friends were impressed and amazed at how quickly I had become successful, but that success came with a price. A price I would soon figure out that I wasn't willing to pay.

I learned quite a bit about management that first year. First and foremost, integrity is something that is lacking in many organizations. It was especially lacking in the decisions of those that I worked with. We had an incident occur where one of our construction projects failed and we had to notify the federal government that we had a major spill of waste material. The spill was fully contained on our property and in the designated disposal area, but it was not planned, and it did interrupt our operations. During the investigation into this spill, I was advised to be very careful with what I said as anything could be used to hit us with large fines, and I could be personally fined if I was found to be culpable.

A $500 raise for that kind of responsibility!? Not worth it. As the investigation continued, I had to escort the investigators around the property. Of course, while I was escorting them, we clearly witnessed our contractors using unapproved and completely unacceptable building methods (unacceptable to the regulatory agencies that is). I couldn't exactly lie to them and tell them they were not seeing what they saw, and when they asked if this was a common practice, all I could say was that they needed to talk to the person in charge of construction, and that wasn't me.

What they were witnessing was obviously a violation of our policies and construction standards, and I was sure the construction manager would have an explanation for them. Of course, I knew that this was our common practice as it was multiple times cheaper to build when you didn't follow code. Not following code probably had something to do with why they were there in the first place.

I will never forget that feeling of having to hide what we were doing as a company. Yes, there was no danger to people in what we were doing but we all knew the risks if we got caught and here, we were, caught. I was losing my integrity on behalf of the company I was working for. I could keep my job and continue to turn a blind eye to our bad practices, or I could find a new job. Trust me, your integrity and security are worth too much to just give them away for your employer. I promised myself that I'd never let myself get into a situation like this again.

31

Later that afternoon, I had to sit in a meeting with the investigators, my boss and our construction manager. The meeting was brief, the investigator started out by asking about our building methods. My boss and our construction manager explained exactly how we went about our construction jobs and our quality control measures. The investigator asked if we ever had instances where we used sub-par practices. He gave a "hypothetical scenario", which happened to be exactly what he had seen earlier. Both my boss and our construction manager said that they had never witnessed this and assured him that it would never occur on our site. My boss went so far as to ask if they were questioning his integrity as we would never reduce our standards to save costs.

I was sick to my stomach, knowing that the investigators KNEW they were being lied to, and having to just sit there and watch. I wish I had had the chance to warn my boss, but then again we all make our own decisions in life, and he made his. We were lucky that the fines were not too bad from that incident, however we had lost every ounce of good will with our regulators and going forward it made life extremely hard.

As a side note, I must confess that in four years working for the company I never once saw us use our approved construction methods. The cost of doing business the right way was simply more than we as a company were willing to pay, which meant rolling the dice and hoping we didn't get caught. Incidentally, the company eventually had to sign a consent decree due to their repeated failures to follow code. This directly led to the business being closed and many people losing their jobs; all due to greed and a lack of integrity.

Integrity and respect can be lost in other more subtle ways too. The year ended with my department being the only department in the company to meet either its production or fiscal budget. We managed to meet both! I had a talk with my boss about how I thought that I had proven that I was capable of performing the job at a high level and that now might be a good time to adjust my salary accordingly. Unbelievably, my boss's response was that he would love to give me a higher salary, but he couldn't have an employee of his making as much or more than him. This absolutely cemented my need to get the hell out of there. I knew that I was being lied to and that my efforts and energy were clearly being wasted.

I was giving up 60 hours a week of my life for this company and my boss, the mine manager, couldn't even be honest with me. Shortly after this conversation I did get a decent raise, but it was for all the wrong reasons. We hired an engineer to work directly for both myself and my counterpart at the Old Hickory Mine. This new engineer had a starting salary that was higher than mine. I figured this out because his salary came out of my budget… I went back to my boss with his same argument and told him, "I can't have an employee making as much or more than me". It worked and I received a $4,000 raise. The only problem was I wasn't going to be sticking around to enjoy the raise.

I needed to work for a company that did business the right way. I was spending 60 hours a week at work plus commuting 35 miles each way and taking calls in the middle of the night several nights a week. This was just not what I had bargained for. So, yet again I found myself in a job where there was no way I would ever "win," and I was stuck on the track of retiring at 59 ½ with my best years behind me.

Chapter 9: Trials and Tribulations of Mining

My remaining time with the company would be short but memorable. First, we had a new employee that was just not working out very well. Hog, yes that was his nickname, had transferred to our department. His previous supervisor had told him not to transfer, because he wouldn't make it in the mine and would end up losing his job.

Hog was just not meant for the physically demanding work of the mine. While his level of effort and willingness to help were admirable, he simply was always in the way. My supervisor, Brett, had to give him his 30-day performance review, and it wasn't going to be pretty. I coached Brett beforehand that he needed to be honest, to the point, and matter of fact. Hog needed to transfer back, or he would be let go at his 90-day review, and Brett needed to get that point across.

Brett's conversation with Hog was honest and to the point. The conversation ended with Hog telling Brett, "I am giving you 110%".

Brett responded with, "I know, it's just that 110% of shit is just more shit". I would have to coach Brett a little more on his bedside manner, but all in all the message had been received and Hog transferred back the next week.

My final unbelievable interaction with our management group was in reporting yet another spill. We were unethically and illegally running our pipeline across an area that we did not have permits for, and within feet of a wetland (hence the not having a permit), and with no spill protection in place. Our pipeline, which was not in the greatest of condition, failed at quitting time one day.

34

I received the call over the radio that we had a break in our pipeline and that there was a spill going into the wetland.

This shit was getting old, why couldn't we just do things the right way? I put on my gear and headed out to the spill site. When I got there the pipeline had already been patched, but there was a massive amount of mud going from our pipeline into the adjacent wetland and pond. The entire wetland was covered in red mud, and the pond water was no longer clear but rather full of mud from our pipeline. I called our environmental manager and informed him that we had had a spill. We'd had more than 15 spills that year.

We were in a real bad place with our regulators due to our history of spills, and our inability to remove the old pipes from service. Our environmental manager asked me how I knew that we had a spill. I responded that it was called in over the radio and that I was at the site, and there was a nice shiny new patch on the pipeline. He proceeded to ask me if I personally saw the mud spilling from our pipeline and flowing into the wetland. I explained that the whole area, including the wetland, was covered in mud. He screamed into the phone to never call him again regarding spills unless we had had an, "actual spill". I was then berated for making assumptions with regards to the origin of this red mud. I was to report only what I had witnessed, and I was not being paid to make assumptions about the origin of red mud that was in a wetland and not on our property. Once again, I was asked if I had personally witnessed the mud flowing out of our pipeline. I responded, "no."

Our environmental manager replied, "good, don't ever call me again unless you can actually confirm a spill," he hung up the phone. This spill would never be spoken of again. My desire to work for a company that did business the right way would forever be ingrained in me. I simply did not want to associate, or be associated with, this type of company ever again.

Experiences like these can really make you want to avoid management roles, and harden you against the type of behavior that you simply can't and won't tolerate. I know now just how important it is to fill your team with individuals of great integrity and character. I also know just how important it is to remove those who would undermine that culture and credence. My tolerance for unethical and illegal behavior is very limited. I know that at times people make mistakes, however the things I experienced at that mine were not mistakes, they were calculated business decisions. Management's myopic views clearly valued short-term profits over anything else. The funny thing is if they would've stepped back, they would've realized that they were sacrificing their own personal integrity and reputation to make someone else money. In the end the Company closed and they had to find other jobs. Reputation matters, and I am sure the reputation of their former employer reflected poorly on them.

Chapter 10: Moving Again

As 2008 came to an end, I accepted a position with Mosaic Potash in Carlsbad, New Mexico. Mosaic was by far and away the best employer I would ever work for. They were everything that my previous company wasn't. Mosaic's senior management truly believed that their employees were their greatest assets and did everything possible to take care of them. In return, Mosaic's employees were fiercely loyal.

That loyalty I felt towards Mosaic Potash is something that I carry with me everywhere I go (as demonstrated in the name I chose for my company: Mosaic Properties). At Mosaic Potash, I worked with people of unquestionable character. Our management was full of people who were open and honest with each other and who would hold each other accountable. Decisions were made because they were the right decisions to make, not because they were easy or popular.

Life at Mosaic was great, I loved the job and worked with great people. I learned what management really is: motivating your employees to achieve their fullest potential. Management is not sitting behind a desk crunching numbers, it is the exact opposite. True management is meeting and interacting with your team and your stakeholders. Nothing is more fulfilling than watching your team come together and conquer tasks that seem insurmountable. At Mosaic, we did that often.

Part of being a salaried employee in the mine department at Mosaic meant becoming a member of the mine rescue team. You are not going to advance far in an underground mining company if you aren't willing to put it all on the line to help your fellow miners in times of trouble. Being on the rescue team also gives you a great deal of respect for the dangers of our profession. Our team was made up of 50% union employees and 50% management employees. Once you advanced into senior management roles, you had to give up your spot on the mine rescue team as you no longer had the time to adequately fulfill your commitments to your teammates.

My time on the mine rescue team was beyond valuable. It taught me much needed skills to be able to respond to an emergency, and it also taught me how not to panic but to remain calm and think through difficult situations. Most importantly mine rescue taught me the value of a team. No one person ever had all the answers to solve the complex problems we trained for, but as a team we were usually able to come up with a workable solution. Furthermore, being on the rescue team and having to rely on my teammates for advice and help really taught me a lot about the institutional knowledge that these guys had. As a salaried member of the team my time was limited and my experience in mining was never equal to the hourly guys. They were true teammates and never shied away from teaching me their knowledge of mine rescue and of mining itself. I am forever indebted to those guys.

I spent many hours studying with my teammates and learning from them. The knowledge gained was well beyond just that of a rescue team member. I learned a whole new perspective on work and motivation. I learned what drove these guys. I learned why they looked up to certain supervisors and why they didn't like others. I learned leadership from them. We could always talk openly together and these guys shared with me what they needed and wanted from their leaders. They shared what they believed made someone a great leader. One of my supervisors Kevin who I thought was one of our weaker supervisors turned out to be one of the most respected supervisors from the hourly guys' point of view. However, they didn't all like him in fact many had transferred away from his crew. Even though many of them didn't like him they all respected him and would follow his instructions as they all knew he would do anything for their safety and he would not lead them into harms way in order to save a buck or two. I had always looked at Kevin as one of my weaker supervisors due to his consistently lower production numbers. What I learned from the guys was he was a stickler for the safety rules and wouldn't allow corners to be cut. The other supervisors were getting better numbers because they were willing to look the other way. Some of the guys liked that because when they looked the other way it made their jobs easier. Taking short cuts can really save time and energy. The guys on those crews didn't have to work as hard and got better production numbers. But in the end the guys who had worked for Kevin were our better employees. They had more integrity, and a better work ethic. They may not have made us as much production but they did things the right way.

In Virginia our guys cut every corner possible and it eventually led to the closing of the Mine. In New Mexico, Kevin's guy's may not have made us a fortune, but they certainly never put the health of the Company or their coworkers at risk.

One of the best parts of being in leadership and being on the rescue team was being able to have the mentorship not only from the salaried team but also from the hourly guys. I could go to them later when things were difficult and get their perspective on decisions that I needed to make. It is always worth hearing the opinion of the guys that are actually going to have to *do* the work. I didn't always take their advise but I always listened to it and they knew that and respected that just as I respected their opinions and ideas.

Just after I had advanced out of my role on the mine rescue team, we had a major collapse in the mine. Miraculously, no one was killed or seriously injured in the collapse. In a stroke of luck, our mining area that was totally lost in the collapse was shut down on the day of the collapse for a maintenance outage and no one was in the area working. We did, however, lose about 20% of our equipment.

As soon as we were given permission to resume our mining operations, we were tasked with the challenge of figuring out how to run on 20% less equipment than we were used to having. That evening, I invited my team over to my house to work on developing a plan to get back into operation and continue to hit our production goals. The fact of the matter was that our production goals had not changed, and we still needed to deliver to our customers. That night at my house, our team decided that we'd move from 10 hour shifts to 12 hour shifts, giving us 20% more working hours to counterbalance our 20% loss in equipment.

My counterpart in maintenance and I presented this to our union employees the next morning, and we received not one single complaint! Our people, from management all the way down to hourly, were committed to our collective success and understood what needed to be done. Anyone who has ever worked in a union shop should recognize the miracle here. We changed the schedules of over 200 hourly unionized employees in bid positions with no notice and did not receive a single grievance. After making some adjustments for those who needed considerations around things such as childcare, we were on our way. Needless to say, not one employee missed a single hour of pay in this transition. While managers at other companies may have been bracing themselves for backlash in a situation like this, I never received so many supportive phone calls in my life. Everyone wanted to know what they needed to do to help. From procurement to human resources to even our regulators it was a real team effort to get the mine back up and running. To make this success even more amazing was that at the time of the collapse our Mine Manager my boss had a death in the family and left for two weeks. He trusted me and my counter part to get things right while he was away. His bosses trusted us as well. No-one second guessed our decisions or tried to jump in and take over. It was really impressive how we relied on the next man up and we were able to be successful because the next man up was adequately trained, and well supported.

Mosaic didn't have some secret sauce to make this possible, they simply had a committed and consistent culture of strong leadership, disciplined hiring practices and ethics. The payoff associated with the loyalty that this kind of environment brings, can and will pay dividends again and again. I was truly humbled to witness and be a part of our "all hands on deck" approach.

In the end, no one tried to place blame, everyone just worked to get things up and running again. There would be a time for finding out the cause of the collapse later, but for the time being we all understood we just needed to focus on getting back into operation, and we did.

Chapter 11: Starting to Invest

The best part of working for a company that knows how to consistently run smoothly is the opportunity to proactively plan. Part of my job was to assist in the development of our long term planning. While I planned for Mosaic's future, I took the opportunity to plan for my personal future as well. It's true, Mosaic gave me a refreshed level of confidence in the notion that companies could do good business and make good money doing it. However, deep down I still knew that I needed to create something of my own. At the time, the economy was recovering, and real estate could be purchased for pennies on the dollar. To top it off, Parham and I both had good paying jobs and hadn't started a family yet. We were ready to invest.

One of the most important parts of real estate investing is location, and I knew that Carlsbad was not the right location for me to invest in. Carlsbad was a small town in a remote part of the country. Neither Parham nor I could see ourselves raising our family there, which was a tough realization as we both enjoyed our jobs. Even so, we kept our end goal in our sights and looked at properties back in Virginia where we had purchased our first house. We knew the area well and were comfortable buying there as we still had family and friends in that area. We also knew that we would be returning there every year and could write off our travel as a business expense. This is just one of the many tax benefits of owning your own company.

In 2011 we purchased two properties in Virginia. Both of these properties needed work, but we were up for the challenge. These new projects were within two blocks of our old house, which we had managed to successfully rent out. While these properties didn't make us any money, they did help us start to learn something that's invaluable when starting a company: what not to do.

My father had agreed to help with managing the rehabs. This turned out to be a blessing for us and a curse for him as we clearly had no idea upfront how much effort rehabs could be. We thought it would be as easy as hiring a flooring guy for floors, a plaster guy for plaster, etc. What no one tells you is that unless you define a subcontractor's work down to the smallest of details, what you get is all the big items done and none of the small things that drain your time and money.

Sure, you would think that the guy installing the ceiling fan would put in light bulbs, but trust me if it's not spelled out for him, he won't. Perhaps the plumber that is installing the toilets, sinks and shower would be able to address the non-functioning shut off valves while he was doing his work? Nope! He just turns off the main and does exactly what the contract says, nothing more. This is where you need to actively manage your projects, and Dad did a great job of this, but it would take up a lot more of his time than we'd planned for. I still can't believe how much effort my Dad put forth on those properties and I feel bad about it every time I think about it. Do not do what we did. Dad I still owe you for that, Thank You! Make certain that when you start your first rehab project, you are there every step of the way. That may mean that you might spend significantly more time and money on the first rehab than expected, but it will pay off in the future. This is how you learn about how your contractor's work, and then you can set expectations accordingly. Some contractors need their hands held the whole time, others don't. The ones that don't tend to cost more.

Both properties rented out very quickly to people that were referred to us by friends. This says a lot about the product that was presented. If your properties take a long time to rent, you either don't have the correct product on the market or your price is too high. I have found that quality properties don't last long on the market, in fact they will rent faster and for more money than others on the same street.

Once the rehabs were completed and the monthly rents started coming in, I was convinced that we had found the solution to getting out of the Rat Race and retiring before the age of 59 ½. That gold watch was going to have to be for someone else. My boss, Terry, by far one of the best people that I ever worked with, once asked me why I would ever want to own rental properties. He just couldn't understand ever wanting to deal with tenants. This is the same person who once said in a meeting, "I will see your 8 years of experience and raise you 35". Terry was a great leader, and he loved working for Mosaic so much so that he just couldn't understand anyone ever wanting anything else in life. Terry was in his 70's and still not talking about retirement. He loved working there so much he couldn't even contemplate the idea of retirement. I, however, was already worried about retirement, and when it would arrive. My goal has always been to be retired by age 40. I want to truly live more of my years than I work, that is my goal in life.

As we continued on with our jobs for several months, the rentals became more and more a part of our life. We made spreadsheets to track revenue, costs and project future returns. I started to calculate how many rentals we would need to own before we would be able to be financially independent. The number was originally 15, owned free and clear, however this number changed like the wind. The more I tried to figure out how to get to 15 properties, the more I figured out that with some minor lifestyle tweaks we could get the number down to 14, or perhaps even 13. I was so committed to achieving financial freedom that I started tracking our spending as if every dollar that we spent was one less dollar that we had to put towards getting out of the Rat Race.

Once our first child, Wyatt, was born, I figured out that each diaper cost us about $0.24, and each wipe was 1.2 cents. I made a mental note every time I changed his diaper on just how much it cost. Kids really are expensive! I may have gone a little overboard with cost cutting, but I understood where our money was going and how much we would need in order to sustain our lifestyle. When you can graph where you are and where you need to be it is very powerful. I knew now, more than ever, that each dollar I could hang onto would bring my retirement date that much closer.

By now we were in fall of 2011, and we owned four rental properties. I had been promoted again at work and was back to those 60+ hour work weeks. Mosaic was great about doing their best to minimize the impact of the 60 hour work week, but it was still a 60 hour work week. Frequently the long days would end with a meeting at a nice restaurant to help alleviate some of the burden. Other times we would cater working lunches, there were even times that I held meetings at my house so that I could spend a little more time with Parham and our new baby, Wyatt. The team really worked well together and no one, other than myself, really seemed to mind the work load. My teammates that didn't mind the incredible hours all had a couple of things in common: they were perfectly fine with working late into their lives and they didn't seem to have any hobbies or interests outside of work. Most of them simply loved working for Mosaic and didn't ever see themselves doing anything else. As an employer, this is what you set out to achieve, and you do it by treating people as if they are your single most valuable asset.

For me, weekends tended to be the worst as we were in an on-call rotation and when it was your weekend you pretty much lived on the computer. During one of my last on-call weekends, I received 95 work related emails, truly unacceptable in my book, but par for the course for an upper management position.

Projecting income from the rental properties, along with the tax benefits, became a real hobby. I never could have imagined how fulfilling it was to be working on a plan to free myself. My dreams of traveling the country and enjoying the national parks would not have to wait until I was old and gray. I would indeed be able to be there to help raise our kids and not just provide for them. I want to be able to instill in our children that life is not about money, it is about what you do with it. I want to be able to do the things in life that I value, and that give meaning and importance to our lives. The problem is I can only do those things if I am financially independent. Having a defined path moving forward, excited and inspired me more than ever, I knew what I had to do reach my goal of being financially independent by the age of 40. All that was left to do was execute.

The first part of that execution involved a trip home for Christmas, a 26 hour drive of over 2,000 miles. That comes out to about a $1,000 tax write off in mileage alone. How about that, getting paid to go on vacation? During our trip home, I had a list of about 15 houses for sale that I wanted to look at. The biggest requirement for a property to be on the list was that it needed to be in rent ready condition, as I now knew that long distance rehabbing was not practical. I could not ask someone to do that for me again, and without someone on site the logistics of managing a rehab was just not something I wanted to do. Location was also important, I wanted to stay in the same school district. There were some pretty bad school districts nearby, and a good school district always attracts better tenants.

After looking at several properties that just were not quite rent ready, or were just too high priced, we found one that was perfect. It hit all of the right criteria: rent ready, newer mechanical systems, great location next to the local school and most of all, motivated sellers. The current owner was retired and living in Florida, and the previous tenant had caught the kitchen on fire. Their insurance company had just completed a $40,000 renovation on the house. It was in perfect condition with refinished hardwood floors, new kitchen floors and all new appliances. To make things even better, the motivated seller had never seen the finished product, or spent any of their own money on the repairs so they were not concerned about recouping the cost of the renovation.

The beauty of motivated sellers is that money is not necessarily the motivator, as was the case here. This seller was motivated by the fact that his asset was becoming a liability and costing him time. The seller had spent considerable time dealing with a displaced tenant, insurance companies, general contractors and now a realtor. As investors, this is where we come into play and we solve problems. This person's problem was that they wanted to be retired and not dealing with an out of state rental property. I was more than happy to make them an offer that would solve their problem and at the same time accomplish my goals of finding a rent ready property that would be a profitable long term investment.

This would be our first property financed as a rental property with a conventional loan. We went the traditional route and applied for a loan with one of the major banks. This turned out to be a real headache that we would never repeat. I discovered that the big banks are not in the business of giving loans to people with multiple properties. Their people are not trained well enough to make the process run smoothly. Also, their processes are not streamlined for people with multiple properties and income streams. We ended up missing our closing date, even with a contract that gave 45 days to close. This was solely due to the banks, loan officers and underwriters not knowing what documents they would need. Our loan officer came to us at the last minute and told us that the underwriter had kicked the file back due to a missing document. Once we got them that document, it got kicked back again due to yet another missing document. This went on through many iterations, chewing up a minimum of two days every time; one day for the underwriter to review, and one day for the loan officer to tell me they needed another document.

I still cannot imagine why the underwriter stops their review immediately upon finding a document missing and sends the file back to the loan officer without completing the review. I would think that it would save a lot of time if the underwriting process could involve a review of the whole file and the sending of a list of all documents that were missing. I am sure there is some quota associated with the number of files they review a day that impacts their incentive structure. So, we play this game where a single file may be sent back and forth multiple times, which senselessly leads to angry customers and missed deadlines.

I have since found that the smaller local banks and commission-paid mortgage brokers give far superior customer service, and many of them specialize in giving loans to investors. They too have discovered that big banks are not good at this and they have raced to fill the void in the marketplace.

Commission-paid mortgage brokers can be a real friend, they only get paid for loans that close. They won't waste their time if the loan is not going to go through. They also don't want to spend their time chasing underwriters, so they are extremely thorough in putting the initial package together. Simply put they won't waste your time or theirs.

Back to the smaller local banks. They really are a great resource. They tend to know the local market and often are mandated to invest their funds into the local community. See when a bank loans you their money, they are investing in you, just as you are investing in a property. Some of these banks really do look at real estate investors as partners. The bank needs to invest (lend out) their money. That is how they make money. If a bank doesn't loan anything out it can't make money. The bank makes money on the interest they charge you. Remember they are paying you interest on your deposits, the difference in interest rates that they charge you versus what they pay you is their profit. (This is an overly simplistic view but it should get the point across). The bank needs people to loan money too. Your bank wants you to be successful as an investor as your success makes them money. The more successful you are the more money they are able to lend to you, and the more money they are able to make.

Additionally, you are going to need to have a business banking account and building a long term banking relationship is essential. It makes things a little easier when your bank is also your mortgage holder. On a personal note, the majority of our notes are held by a local co-operative bank. They sponsor our local investor association Great Lakes REIA. They specialize in business loans to investors. Sure, they make other loans all banks do, but they know your business and that is important. You need a partner that knows your business. Local banks have been that partner for us. If you are looking for an investor friendly bank, go to a REIA meeting and find out what banks are there, and make friends with them. That relationship will help you for years to come.

Now back to the newest property to our real estate investment portfolio. Our rent ready house was in need of a tenant. This part of the process went amazingly well. One of our current renters referred someone to us who turned out to be a good quality candidate. Most referrals are good candidates, who wants to refer someone that would make them look bad? The timing also worked out well as we were back in New Mexico when the purchase closed. The new tenant was able to pick the key up from the closing company and move into the property the very day it closed. It has been over five years and I haven't stepped foot into that house since we made the initial offer. The house has been continuously rented since we took possession of it. Buying a house in a desirable location and being able to price the rent competitively makes all the difference in the world.

With five rentals now under our belts, my job having expanded to 60 hours a week, Our one year old son Wyatt at home and a daughter on the way, something needed to give. Through my constant analysis of our investments, I figured out that my "hourly wage" coming from the rentals was higher than that of my full-time employment. This was not only a complete affirmation that we were on the right track with real estate investing, but it was also confirmation that my job was holding me back. I could make more in real estate if I had more time to work on it. The only problem was I still needed the paycheck from my full-time job. This is the proverbial catch 22. I just needed a way to tone down the demands of my full-time job to something more manageable thereby allowing me to expand on the investing side.

Fortunately, a friend of mine called me about an engineering manager position at a mine in Ohio. I was very hesitant to move the family again so soon, especially since my wife Parham was pregnant with our second child at the time. Mosaic was a great place to work and it was going to be hard to top that.

I asked the recruiter that I had been referred to if he had ever been to Cleveland, Ohio. When he told me that he lived there, I asked him if it really was as big of a dump as the news would suggest. Jack, the recruiter, was very professional about telling me that it was actually a pretty nice place, but I was far from convinced. We have all seen the "Mistake on the Lake - Cleveland Tourism" video. If you haven't seen it, it ends with, "at least we aren't Detroit!" That told me all I needed to know. I eventually told him that he needed to move on and find someone else as Cleveland, Ohio just didn't appear to be a great place to raise a family. Having seen what was in the news about Cleveland I, nor anyone I knew, was impressed. I wanted my next move to be my last and Cleveland didn't seem like a place to settle down.

Jack kept assuring me that Cleveland was nice. Finally, he made me an offer that I could not refuse. Jack promised me a free all-expense paid vacation to Cleveland if I would just stop by the mine and interview with the management team. He was willing to buy us tickets to the Rock and Roll Hall of Fame and a nice night out on the town. I just needed to show up to the interview. Jack made a bold bet that if he could just get me to visit Cleveland, it would sell itself. He won his bet. We now live in Cleveland, and there is no chance that we are leaving.

Jack, an astute businessman, took a well calculated risk. He knew what mattered to us and what he had control over. It wasn't the job, he knew I loved my job, it was time and location that were our motivators for entertaining the idea of moving in the first place. Jack made sure we experienced the best of Cleveland on our trip out. Jack also made sure that we would be informed that the job was only 40 hours a week.

Jack won his bet the same way we aim to win our bets on investment properties. He had gotten to know me, his "customer." He knew what I wanted, and knew that if he could deliver, we would make the move. He never tried to sell the job, as he knew he couldn't beat my current situation. In fact, he spent considerable time telling me how messed up the place was and how much they needed leadership and change. They needed someone that had experienced what a well-run facility looked like. In our research on properties, we need to know our "customer," as well as their wants and needs prior to making our investment. Jack knew my needs before he spent his money, hence he made a good bet that paid off. He knew I wanted a challenge and he knew that my wife and I needed a good, safe environment to raise our kids in.

Investing in real estate should be no different than investing in people. After all, it is people who are renting your real estate. You need to know the "customer" that you are looking to attract in order to deliver the product that they require. If you do this, you will win every single time. Knowing your customer not only leads you to the right neighborhoods and properties, but it guides you through the selection process of your rehab and the marketing process on the back end.

Back at Mosaic, I needed to get my life back. I commuted just over 60 miles round trip to work each day and carried a 60 hour work week. Needless to say, the work life balance was just no longer palatable. After quite a bit of back and forth with both my wife and the new employer, I accepted the position in Ohio. I would start after our daughter, Caroline, was born. My wife and I relocated to Cleveland just six weeks after Caroline's birth. The deciding factor in the move was that the new job was promised to be generally 40 hours per week. The mine didn't operate on weekends (or so I was told), and as a non-operations position, I was to focus on long term projects and would not be involved in the day to day. Yet again, I was moving with the hopes of getting my time back and getting the opportunity to better realize my dream of retiring early and leaving the Rat Race. At least this time I had a good plan for exiting the Rat Race. Real estate! As it turns out, Cleveland is one of the best real estate markets in America.

I was really going to miss the team that we had in place at Mosaic. Despite all of the frustrations that I had working for a large company, things were pretty good. The future that I wanted just was not there.

Immediately upon starting my new job in Ohio, I found myself exactly where I hadn't wanted to be: knee deep in day to day operations. One month after I starting as engineering manager, we began demolition of our Tipple Bin and the construction of its replacement.

In underground mining, you mine ore from the bowels of the earth and bring it up to the surface using a massive hoist. In my case, the ore was being mined 2,000 feet below the surface and two and a half miles out underneath Lake Erie. Our hoist had two 1250 horsepower motors that lifted the ore up to the surface of the earth, 17 tons at a time. Underground, the ore is loaded into skips which are essentially large buckets. Once the skip is full, the hoist lifts it to the surface, where it is tipped over and the ore pours into a large bin (the Tipple Bin). This hoist was capable of delivering 17 tons of ore to the tipple bin every 90 seconds. The ropes that are attached to the skips are suspended over an immensely important structure called the Headframe. This is the building which supports the weight of the large steel cables that are attached to the skip. It holds up the weight of the skip, the large cables attached to the skip and the 17 tons of ore that is inside of the skip. It is the single most expensive and important building on a mine site.

Our Tipple Bin had structural degradation that required its immediate replacement. We had hired a major steel erection company to remove the old tipple bin and install a new one. Their workers performing the demolition complained that our Headframe was not safe. This was the adjoining building that towered over the Tipple Bin. The workers were concerned that they had to work underneath this building. They were further upset that it was not being replaced as well.

Apparently, our operational guys were not addressing the contractors concerns properly. Because, eventually the workers performing the demolition grew concerned enough that they went to our union president with their concerns. The union president came to me with the complaint and asked me to investigate.

I was a little annoyed to be playing mediator in an operations versus union disagreement. I could not imagine that there was anything wrong with the Headframe. After all, it is the single most important and expensive building on most mine sites. I knew it had to be in good working order. (I had never seen a Headframe that wasn't in pristine condition. They are like fire trucks always looking perfect.) Our headframe was filthy but come on it had to be in good condition structurally. Up until this job I had never even seen a headframe that was not in near perfect condition. These things are not allowed to fail. Being new to the job I figured it best to start out on the right foot with our hourly workforce. If nothing else, it would set a good precedent that we were going to treat concerns with respect and conduct our business the right way.

After a little research, I decided to call the engineering firm that had recommended the demolition of the old Tipple Bin. I wanted to see if they had looked into the condition of our headframe which was the building in question. After quite a bit of asking around, I found the name of the company that had performed the structural analysis of our Tipple Bin. I was put in touch with the licensed professional engineer that inspected our Tipple Bin. He informed me that we were in possession of his full report and that if I had any concerns, I should read the report. This struck me as both a little unprofessional and rude, but I proceeded to ask one of my engineers for the report. After a substantial amount of digging and prodding, I was able to obtain a copy. I immediately understood why it was so hard to find the report, and why the professional engineer was so short with me. In reading the report, I knew I was in trouble. My new employer was playing with fire and people's lives. I was right back to a place where I had vowed never to put myself again, working for a company that lacked integrity. The report essentially stated that _both_ of the buildings were unsafe to operate, and we were only replacing one of them! To make matters worse, the report was two years old. Can you imagine the consequences if something had happened and the company was found to be sitting on a report stating that the buildings had been deemed unsafe to operate?

Our senior management at both the site level and at the corporate office were aware that our buildings were not structurally sound and did nothing with that information for two years. After 2 years, only one of the two buildings was getting replaced, and there were no plans to address the Headframe... The single most valuable asset at any mine. During those two years, they did not warn their employees of the impending danger or make the required temporary repairs to prevent a catastrophic failure of either building.

I went to my boss and told him about the problem, and his only response was that we only had so much money for repairs and that we were addressing the worst problems first. Unfortunately, once you have documentation that buildings are not safe you need to do something, and this was not an acceptable response or plan in my book. I had to make a formal request for unbudgeted money to get the Headframe temporarily repaired so that we weren't inviting lawsuits and jail time. The money was ultimately approved as a "cost overrun" on the replacement of the Tipple Bin.

I could not believe that our upper management team was putting their bonuses above the safety of our people and the long term viability of our facilities. I needed to get the heck out of this new job, I had jumped out of the pot and into the fire. This company was not healthy, and if major changes didn't happen fast, things were going to get ugly. Your integrity is the one thing people can't take from you, I wasn't going to give mine away to keep the security of a job that was going to potentially land me and my coworkers in jail. I had made a promise to never put myself in a position like this again, and here I was. I needed to expedite my plan B.

The good news was that Parham and I were developing a real passion for real estate investing. We both could see an achievable path to financial independence, we just needed to continue to focus on our investing and tackle the challenges as a team.

Though my wife, Parham, really enjoyed her work, we had talked about her staying home with the kids on many occasions. She just wasn't ready to make that leap yet. Parham had been financially independent since she was 18 and felt a great deal of personal satisfaction in her contributions to the family. Our challenge was that managing and growing our rental property portfolio was something that needed dedicated attention, and that wasn't something either of us was in a position to give.

I needed help managing our growing business, and Parham's natural organizational and detailed-oriented skills made her just the right person for the job. She also loves being a mother and spending time with the kids which is where she is at her finest. It took a few months, but I finally convinced her that if she really needed a "job" (as if being a full-time mom isn't a job) she could run our real estate business. It was becoming obvious that it wasn't going to grow at the rate we required with just me doing the work. Parham wasn't really convinced, but reluctantly she decided to stay home with the kids and run the business full-time. Within two weeks, she had found and purchased a new rental property.

We were now up to a total of six properties, located in both Ohio and Virginia.

Having Parham managing the business was working out well. As for our new property, she had managed to negotiate our ability to have access to the house for showings before closing. This allowed Parham to have a tenant selected prior to taking possession of the property. Closing was on a Monday in mid-December of 2012, and Parham had the new tenant in place on Friday of the same week! None of this would have been possible if we both would have been working full-time while trying to raise a family. Parham's involvement in the business was going to be the key to our success and expansion.

As we entered the new year, Parham continued to take ownership and provide direction for our company. One of her first priorities was to formally start our business. Parham filed for our LLC the first week of January and shortly after that we started our business banking accounts. The Ohio properties would operate under our new business entity.

In filing for our LLC, we learned quite a bit. All the experts advise that you need to get a lawyer to create an LLC for you. That's probably not bad advice, however have you ever looked at what a lawyer's fees would be for this and what you get for your money? Lawyers tend to charge a lot for this service, which really should be quite inexpensive. The paperwork for creating an LLC is fairly simple after you have done it once. You just add a couple names, addresses and dates to an already existing document. How can making those changes justify a $2,000+ lawyer's fee? I hope these lawyers don't believe that we are all naive enough to think that they create a new document from scratch each time. Yes, we didn't get some of the benefits of using a lawyer such as anonymity, but we did get to keep another $2,000 in our accounts to grow our business with.

Parham did quite a bit of research and found all the required documents to create our LLC online. She did everything herself, and while it may not have been as pretty as hiring it out, the job got done and we saved about $2,000. Remember, the easiest way to have money is not spending it when you get it. This can be a very expensive business when you contract everything out. Be self-sufficient, it will pay off in the long run, just don't be cheap. There is a difference. Now that our business has grown and we have better cashflows, we do use lawyers a lot more often, but at the critical time of getting your business growing, cash matters and you need to be careful with it. (Note, after joining our REIA we found a lawyer that would create LLC's for a very reasonable rate. One of the benefits of a REIA is finding the right partners)

We have found that taking the advice of others can be very expensive. Other people (especially so-called experts and guru's) have no problem spending your hard-earned money. I advise that you take some time to really look at how these experts run their businesses and see how they spend their money. People tend to say one thing but do another when it comes to their own funds. A lot of experts give advice that they don't practice. Be wary.

Now that we officially had a business, we needed a business bank account. In starting our business banking accounts, we went with one of the big banks that advertises nationally. This seemed like a no brainer, but we still managed to screw it up.

Turns out those big banks that advertise "small business loans made easy" will find a reason not to loan to *your* small business. They loan to small businesses that are very well established, not start-ups, and certainly not real estate investing start-ups. What those banks are really looking for are deposits. They are not really looking to give out loans to you. Read their financial reports and see where they actually make their money.

The bank that we went with had told us all about their small business loan programs and their great business checking programs. Their offerings really were great, the only problem was they forgot to tell us that they don't lend to businesses that don't have at least two years of tax returns. Our no brainer decision was not going to work for us. What a big waste of time and energy. Another lesson learned the hard way. I had even gone a step further and had switched our personal accounts to this new bank thinking that we were consolidating everything and were streamlining our personal and business lives.

Eventually, we found a great local bank. A local cooperative bank, they are a perfect fit. They are sponsors of our local real estate investment association (Great Lakes REIA), and fully understood what we wanted to do with our business and how they could help. The staff was friendly, but better yet they were very familiar with people in our position. They were there to offer advice and assistance in setting up the right kind of accounts. Best of all, they were willing to give loans to investors like Parham and I. They didn't loan just to "small" businesses that happened to have millions in sales and years of business experience, but to real people who were trying to start and grow businesses. Moving all of our accounts over yet again was a real pain, but in the end it was worth it to get to the right place with the right business partner. When you make a mistake, correct it quickly and move on.

The lesson that we learned here was that the local banks are more willing to invest in the community, as they understand the local economy better. Our bank knew the local investing market, actively attended trade group meetings and was comfortable in doing business with people that were trying to run their businesses the right way. Their loan process was more about people and not necessarily a blanket rejection due to being a start-up. If the underlying people who owned the business were good and were qualified, then they were willing to loan.

Using a local bank offered us the opportunity to be considered to receive a loan, while some of the big banks wouldn't even accept our loan applications. With our local bank we still had to be qualified when applying for a loan, but we didn't have to jump through impossible hurdles. Local banks ultimately have the same or higher standards as big banks, they just don't have as rigid of rules. Bureaucracy there tends to be less, which is good for us small business owners and real estate investors. Note that as you grow your business, you may reach a point that you do need to move to a more specialty bank. We learned that the hard way once we no longer had W-2 employment. Our Co-operative bank is a great bank, but they have certain debt to income thresholds. Most banks do, but as a Co-Op bank they are a little more conservative. There are banks out there that will lend based on the property you are buying and not based on your income. When you hit the point in your business that those are the problems you are facing, just know that you have done pretty well for yourself. Also know there are more resources available to you at that point than banks, banks are always the most obvious solution but once you are established there are many sources of private money. Also know that there will be a point in the future that you will be big enough and successful enough to go back to your local bank. Relationships matter don't burn your bridges.

Chapter 12: Learning to Landlord

Less than two months after we closed on our first Ohio property, Parham found another one. As it turns out, women are really good at buying things. This house was a very nice three-bedroom, one bath house that was part of an estate. The estate was being ran by the son who lived just down the street, and he didn't want to sell the house. However, he was not able to fix it up either. He wanted to fix it up, I just don't think he knew where to begin. This is a problem that a lot of people face, they are still attached to a home and struggle to motivate themselves to get it ready to sell. The son had removed all of the furniture except for a sofa and a TV. He would stay at the home watching TV most evenings, when he was supposed to be fixing it up. Eventually, the son recognized that he had a problem and that the house needed to be sold. Luckily, we were there to help him with his problem. We made a fair offer on the home and now we were heading to seven rental properties.

Upon inspection of the home, we found that the son had not touched the forty years' worth of belongings in the attic, and he had not emptied out any of the sheds. We were able to make an offer that gave piece of mind to the son and alleviated him of the problem of going through the remainder of the memories left in the attic and shed. Again, our offer was fair, but it was discounted due to the service that we were providing. Additionally, we agreed to rehab and finish the house to a premium condition. An interesting side note is that after the purchase was complete the son never came by the house to see the progress even one time. Knowing that his childhood home was in good hands, and would be well taken care of allowed him to finally move on.

Once we started the renovation, things went quick. We installed all new flooring throughout the house, and updated all ceiling fans, lights and hardware. It did not take very long or cost very much money to make a huge difference in the appearance and appeal of the home. One of my main concerns with the house was the pastel pink bathroom. The 1950's tub and sink were pink, as well as the tub surround. Luckily, during the renovation, we received a flyer for a home remodeling exposition. Against my better judgement, we went to the trade show. It was a real experience. There were companies of every type there, selling every product imaginable.

My problem was that none of these companies were advertising to investors. They were all there to sell to the general public at retail prices. Retail prices tend to be significantly above the costs us investors and rehabbers can afford to pay and still make money. My big take away from the trade show was that tilework and tubs didn't always have to be replaced, they could be resurfaced. I couldn't believe it, here was the solution to my bathroom problem! I no longer needed to replace the tub, which would have been a big ordeal. Parham found out all about the refinishing process and how it worked. The following Monday, Parham contacted about five companies that specialized in tub refinishing and we ended up using one that had not been advertising at the show. This tub resurfacing company was willing to charge wholesale rates to investors, and we ended up getting the job done for about a one third reduced fee compared to any of the companies advertising at the trade show.

Once the resurfacing work was completed, it looked like a brand new tub and sink. I couldn't believe just how much of a transformation was made with such a minimal cost. Better yet, we were able to save money on the bathroom portion of our renovation budget which was good because I had not estimated costs well for all of the new hardware that was required throughout the house.

As the inside of the house was finishing up, it was time to start on the yardwork. One of the problems with estates, and rehab properties in general, is that the yards have usually gone years without very much attention. This property was in serious need of some landscaping. Over half of the back yard was filled with ivy and thorn bushes. Small trees had started to grow near the foundation of the house as well as all throughout the yard. We went ahead and started advertising the house even with the yard in such poor condition.

There was a significant amount of interest in the house and we ended up selecting the perfect tenants. It was obvious that the new tenants had good character and that they wanted to be a part of the community. The husband had grown up just down the street and knew many of the neighbors. He was also very handy and more than willing to take on the yard as it would give him and his wife a nice project to work on together. Incredibly, these tenants still live in the house and have made a significantly positive impact on the property. They took care of the yard work and truly transformed the property from a house to a home.

The new tenants did not have perfect backgrounds, in fact their backgrounds were far from perfect. Both Mike and Nikki were very upfront about this and went on to share what they were doing to get their lives back on track (including attendance at AA meetings). The wife was a recovering drug addict and the husband was a recovering alcoholic. Both talked openly about their recovery and how much better their lives were now.

After reviewing all of the applications, we ended up going with them. Sometimes it is better to go with the enemy that you know versus the one that you don't know. We knew what their problems were, and we knew that they were committed to addressing them. It has been several years since they moved into this house and they have never missed a payment or been late. Furthermore, they maintain the house perfectly. They have truly made it their home and it has been a rewarding experience for everyone involved.

I was once at the house for maintenance, and Mike was there with his dad. He had picked him up from the nursing home to spend an afternoon with him. Mike mentioned that while his dad was not always there for him, he was committed to being there for his dad. I think he figured that if he was not there for his dad when he needed him, then he was no better of a person than his dad had been. He was committed to being his best self. This is truly the kind of tenants that we should all strive to have in our rental properties. Both Mike and Nikki spend considerable amounts of their personal time and money helping recovering addicts. The countless hours that they volunteer contribute greatly towards building a stronger community. In buying this rental property, we not only improved a single derelict property, we were also able to help improve the character of the neighborhood. We don't place just anyone in our properties, we place good quality people in good quality homes. This home was getting its second chance and so were the tenants. Neither has disappointed.

Parham and I have found that when selecting tenants, you should not use blanket policies such as not renting to felons, people with drug convictions, or people with histories of bankruptcy. Tenants come from all walks of life and have had life experiences that most of us couldn't ever imagine. It is really hard to try and fit each person into certain categories. I place a lot of weight on a person's character and work ethic. Don't focus entirely on their past as many of us have made mistakes in life. Focus on what your prospective tenants are doing to correct those mistakes and how they are making right of the things that they have done wrong. Looking at people this way will tell you more than you can imagine about them. It will also tell you whether or not they have truly learned from their mistakes, and if they are likely to repeat them. You will make some mistakes with this method, but I have found that it works out pretty well in the long run. More often than not, we have ended up with good long term tenants using this approach. We have also managed not to get into the crosshairs of fair housing groups.

Looking at applicants this way is a good way to stay out of trouble with the various fair housing groups. Those organizations really frown on you simply ruling out whole groups of people based on things such as past felony convictions. They view this as just another type of discrimination. Groups such as felons are disproportionately minority and having policies that prevent them from renting properties has historically been one way of keeping minorities out of rental properties. These more subtle policies are now starting to draw significant attention, as we as a society are becoming more conscious of our actions. Whether you agree or disagree with that assessment is irrelevant as the government is starting to agree with it more and more. This does not mean that we should just allow anyone into our properties, we still need to do our due diligence and maintain our standards. As landlords we do, however, need to avoid blanket policies. Many professional landlords now use a decision matrix to rank potential tenants. Using a well-designed matrix is a great way to avoid discriminating. It also gives you considerable standing if you are ever accused of discrimination. Having the data to prove that you are doing business the right way is critical. Documentation showing your nondiscriminatory tenant selection practices can prove instrumental in a legal setting. Having this data can also be very useful outside of the court setting.

I once had a minority couple apply for a house that was in an affluent neighborhood that was mostly Caucasian. I also had several other applicants, one of which was more qualified and many that were less qualified. When we informed the various applicants that they were not selected for the house, there were some complaints.

The first complaint was from a group of three unmarried males that wanted to live in the house together. After meeting them the first time, it was obvious that it was not a good fit. One was talking about where the pool table would go the other was planning the location for his beer fridge while the third was asking if he could make improvements to the home's electrical system for discounted rent. Needless to say, they were not selected. When they asked why they hadn't been selected, I was able to simply and accurately state that one of the members of this group scored exceedingly low on the decision matrix. In fact, he was the lowest score we had ever received. The applicant had a low 400 credit score, multiple judgements on file and numerous delinquent accounts. The other two guys were not happy, but they understood that they were rejected based on fact and not based on familial status (or lack thereof) or the belief that they would be bad tenants. They were rejected because they could not pass the background requirements that we had in place.

The other complaint was from the minority couple. That couple was very qualified, but the fact of the matter was that they were not the most qualified. I was able to share with their real estate agent that they had lower credit scores than the couple we selected, and that they also had higher revolving credit balances as well as less income than the couple that we went with. These were all facts that couldn't be disputed. They were not opinions or gut feelings. They were indisputable facts.

It is easy to feel discriminated against when someone cannot articulate why you were not selected, especially when you were well qualified. I believe that the couple's feeling of discrimination went away when we were able to show how we had come to our decision, and what we had considered. If we would not have been able to articulate our reasoning, there is a good chance that we would have ended up in front of the licensing board. Believe me, if you ever get hauled off to court or a licensing board you want facts and you want them to clearly frame your reasoning as valid and impartial.

Chapter 13: Adding Wind to the Sails

After purchasing our seventh investment property, the last two of which in only a few months span, we took a little bit of time to allow the finances catch up and the rents to stabilize. It is good to take a little breather every now and then to make sure that you are able to keep up with the added workload that each property brings. We were still able to keep up, however Parham was starting to realize that now, more than ever, this really was a job for her. It no longer looked like a hobby, and the income every month, as well as the expenses, were very real. There was a lot to keep track of.

Work continued forward for me, things were never truly stable. We just seemed to move from one crisis to another. Work had started off the year with the crisis of very strong sales, and a workforce that was recovering from several months of being laid off. Our company was under relatively new ownership, and I was part of a team that was running various strategic investment scenarios. This new project meant that I had to spend a week in Canada at our regional headquarters.

I was excited for the opportunity to finally meet some of the people at the corporate office that I had been working with and to see what the headquarters was like. I imagined it to be some sort of high rise located downtown, or possibly a low rise building with the name of our business in bold letters on the side. I had lots of time to daydream about the building, the people that I would meet and our project, since we were forced to drive over 12 hours each way in an effort to save money on airfare. That should really tell you something about the mindset of our senior leaders right there. It turned out that our headquarters was in a small office building across the highway from a shopping mall in the outer suburbs. Nothing exciting at all. I am not sure if we even had our name on the building.

Once we had checked into the regional headquarters, we were assigned to a meeting room that would serve as our office for the rest of the week. It was just down the hall from our Vice President of Operations. I was excited to meet our Vice President of Operations. I had been introduced to him while interviewing for my position, but I had never really met him. Turns out I would find out everything I needed to know about our vice president without ever meeting him. We spent three days at the regional headquarters and had a total of 2 hours of face time with anyone other than our project group. We did get lunch with our director, which did not go well. Our project group and the director sat down for lunch next to the vice president who apparently was not in a good mood. He didn't speak one word to any of us during the meal, never so much as even acknowledging our presence. At one point, our director tried to introduce us to him. He quickly ended the introduction with a very annoyed glare as he stood up and walked away. Everyone in the group was pretty taken aback, after all he was the one who had required us to drive 12 hours to meet with him.

In the end, the meeting turned out to be essentially a complete waste of time. Our group accomplished very little during the week. We spent Monday driving 12 hours to the meeting, and Tuesday trying to get our computers to access to the network (Really should not take an entire day but we had no IT staff at the facility). Wednesday was the first day that we were able to actually work, and after our lunch meeting that day no one was particularly motivated. Thursday was supposed to be set aside for meetings with senior management and reviewing our work. Unfortunately, the only member of senior management that we met with was our director. That meeting was about an hour long and consisted entirely of how to report on the status of the new monthly performance goals for our site. Not one word was mentioned about the project that had taken us away from our families for the week. Friday morning, we woke up early and made the 12 hour drive home.

Again, another experience that left me wondering why I was giving so much of my time and life to others. This was an entire week that was spent away from my family, for essentially no reason at all. Working for others, especially people that don't value you or your precious time, is just simply uninspiring. Not only did I miss that week with my family, but I'd be missing more time with them as I was now a week behind back at the office and had to put in extra hours to get caught back up. Who and what was I doing this for? This management team was not inspiring or even motivating. They did not know how to lead. Much to my dismay, it was clear that this experience was eerily similar to what I had experienced earlier in my career and swore to never repeat.

Chapter 14: The Learning Curve

Back on the real estate investing front I was getting more motivated than ever. I really needed to find a job that was fulfilling. It was hard not to buy something or take an expensive vacation to get my mind off the mundane activities of work, but we were very disciplined in our spending. Making things harder in that department was the fact that Parham and I had just inherited a little bit of money. We resisted the temptation to spend it or to splurge on a new car. We decided to put that money to work for us.

In the fall of 2013, we were back to work looking for investment properties. We identified two properties of interest. The first property we looked at was just perfect. The previous owner had been renovating it as a retirement project, when he got sick and passed away. The house was almost completely renovated but was not quite finished. The other property was a bank owned property.

This bank owned property was in pretty rough shape. When we went to view the house, our realtor opened the front door, and promptly gagged, turned around and said she was done looking. The odor pouring out of the house was god-awful. The house reeked of cat urine and feces. My wife was hanging out with the little ones in the car and when she saw the realtor's face, she was ready to leave as well.

So here I was, standing in front of the open door to the house. I told the realtor, "I drove all the way here I might as well look inside." She said to go ahead, she would be in the car. The house smelled so bad I could hardly stand it, but everything in the house seemed in pretty good condition. This house didn't really need that much work, obviously the smell needed to be dealt with. The flooring was all ruined, however the windows were newer, the cabinets were in good shape and best of all the floor plan was excellent.

I walked out of the house, and Parham and the realtor were sitting in the car. They were clearly both in shock that I had actually managed to walk through the house. The realtor was half joking that I needed to check myself for fleas. Parham was upset that I was going into a house like that and then expecting to get into her car. Our oldest was in the backseat yelling "stinky house, stinky house!" Once I told them that I liked the house and that I would take it, they both looked at me in shock. I told them they should check it out, the floor plan was really good and the house was generally in good condition other than the terrible smell. The realtor said she would write an offer if I wanted her to, but she would not be going in to look at the house. Parham agreed with her, except for the writing an offer part. She informed me that this project would be all my mine. I agreed that I would take care of getting the smell out of the house.

Time for the offer. The house was listed at $35,000, and we offered $32,500 for the house. Two days later I received a call from the realtor that the bank was counteroffering us at $28,500. This made no sense whatsoever; maybe they had found out about the smell? Who was I to argue? I begrudgingly accepted their counteroffer at $4,000 below our original offer. Still to this day I can't figure out the circumstances behind that. I just chalk that up to shrewd negotiating. Most of the major banks are not set up to be real estate owners, and their processes for foreclosure and liquidation of real estate are inefficient. To tell you the truth, most of our bank experiences are arduous. We have made offers on numerous banked-owned properties that didn't go through. Many times, the failure is due to the extended process that the banks have in place regarding receiving, responding to and reacting to offers. Many banks want to take up to two weeks to respond to an offer and then they turn around and tell you that you have 48 hours to get them all of the information that they are requesting, or their acceptance will be rescinded. I suspect some of this delay is an effort to see if any other offers may be forthcoming on the property in an attempt to start a bidding war.

This multiple offer situation is one of my pet peeves. You make an offer on a property, only to find out that apparently half the state has also made an offer and the bank then asks you for your "highest and best offer." This way they can play the parties against each other to push the price up. This has happened to us so many times that I have to wonder how truthful it is that there truly are other offers. Several times I have offered on houses that have been on the market for over 180 days, with no accepted offers. However, as soon as I make my offer, I find myself in a multiple offer situation. What are the odds that this house that needs significant work, and has not received an acceptable offer in 180 days suddenly has two or more offers on it? I would be less skeptical if there had just been a price reduction or something like that, however that rarely is the case. In the end, we rarely ever change our offer when we are in a multiple offer situation. If we do change our offer, it is usually only by a very slight amount.

On another occasion, we offered on a house that was a short sale. The occupant had not made a payment on the house in over two years but had agreed to a "cash for keys" program. The deadbeat homeowners would be paid $3,500 to turn in the keys to the house and move out once the sale went through. Up until that time, the bank would allow them to live in the house and not foreclose on it. To me this seems like making a deal with the devil, as the occupants had already stolen two years' worth of mortgage payments. Now the bank was offering to give these people $3,500 to move out. What could go wrong?

A couple of weeks prior to closing, the bank sold the mortgage to another major bank. This new bank did not believe in the cash for keys program and had notified the owner/occupant of this. Sometime during our offer process, the occupant decided that he was not going to move out without being paid. Can you imagine demanding $3,500 to move out of a house that you had not made a payment on in over two years? What a piece of work. That, my friends, is why the first bank should have simply foreclosed on him from the get-go. The "owner" of the property was no longer willing to sell the property that he had not made any payments of for over two years. He owed over $75,000 more than the house was worth and was demanding to be paid to cooperate in the selling/foreclosure process. As far as I was concerned, the deal was dead once the guy refused to move out and sign the documents to sell the house. What a waste of time and effort.

I received a phone call over six months later from my realtor that the bank and "owner" were willing to accept our offer. They just had one small stipulation, I had to close within 14 days. I countered them that I was willing to close in 14 days, but my initial offer from over six months earlier was being reduced by $2,000. The bank balked and the deal fell apart. The bank that was taking a massive haircut on the property to the tune of over $75,000 walked over a $2,000 difference in price… Over two years later, the house finally came up for sale as a bank-owned property. I went and looked at it again and I was glad that the deal had fallen apart. The house was in terrible condition. Several of the floor joists were broken and a roof leak had caused considerable sheet rock damage. I didn't even bother to make an offer on it. Like all homes, it did eventually sell. The final selling price was just under half of what I had initially offered almost three years earlier.

Back at our new $28,500 investment property, things were moving forward. I did a final walk through of the house the day before closing and found the source of some of the smell. The laundry room of the house was about 8 feet wide with a washer, dryer and hot water tank lined up from wall to wall. The washing machine was sitting in the corner tight up against one wall and about 4 inches out from the back wall. The dryer was sitting directly adjacent to the washing machine and was also set about 4 inches from the back wall. Finally, there was the hot water tank that was tightly fit between the dryer and the exterior wall of the house. When I looked behind the dryer to see if it was gas or electric, I found the source of the smell. Piled up two feet high and running the entire width of both the washing machine and dryer was the biggest pile of cat shit anyone has ever seen. I threw up in my mouth right then and there. This was one of the most disgusting things I have ever found in a house.

The next day was our anniversary. In a true celebratory fashion, Parham got a house and I got a pile of crap to clean up. We closed on the house in the morning, and after I changed the locks that afternoon, we went out and had a nice dinner to celebrate being one property closer to financial independence. I don't know why I was so insistent on changing the locks right away, as if there was any chance anyone was going into that house to steal anything. No self-respecting thief would walk into that place.

That weekend was one long and painful clean up. I hauled the appliances to the scrap yard to get rid of them, none of them were worth salvaging. Next, I shoveled the cat poop into trash bags, removed the remaining carpet and scrubbed all surfaces of the house. This is when I discovered a new and exciting location of cat poop: on top of the cabinets. I have never been a cat person, but now I am really not a cat person. What absolute filth, and to think that people had been living in this house with that going on and not doing anything about it. The thought makes my skin crawl. In investing, you will find many things that make your skin crawl, but this has got to be up there on the list. Once the inside of the house was clean, I opened up the crawl space to change the filter in the furnace. Lo and behold, even more cat poop. A catastrophic (pun intended) amount of poop totaling at least 20 large piles. How this could've happened is beyond me. The crawl space was sealed and could only be accessed from a trap door in the living room floor. I guess when they got tired of the cat pooping inside the house, they would throw it in the crawl space as punishment? I don't know, but either way that house was disgusting.

Luckily for us some people live like that, and that is how we as investors can make a considerable amount of money. Once cleaned up, my $28,500 house was pretty respectable. I now just had to paint the entire house to get rid of the smell. I put two coats of oil-based primer over every surface in the house. The ceiling, exposed wood trim, walls, doors and subfloor all received two coats of oil-based paint. Next, I had to paint the house with regular paint, which went significantly slower than the oil-based painting. You see with the oil-based paint, I didn't need to worry about getting wall paint on the trim or trim paint on the walls. I had one mission, and that was to put oil-based odor blocking paint on everything. Once everything had been coated with this odor-blocking technology, the smell was finally gone. Unless you knew better, you would never have been able to tell that there had been an odor problem in the house. I could now bring Parham over to see the inside of the house for the first time. When she saw it she really liked it, which was good because we were stuck with it.

As the renovation progressed, we closed on the other house that we had looked at (the one that was 90% rehabbed already). This presented me with a real problem, there was one of me and two houses that needed work. I decided to switch over and finish the rehab on this new house, as it was almost complete. Besides, a change of scenery would be nice. If I had any brains at all, I would have contracted all of the painting out but at this point in our real estate investing we were still doing everything that we could to conserve cash so that we could have it for future purchases.

The new house, while much more expensive, only needed the closet doors framed in and new appliances. This was a pretty easy task, but it did take some time. The closet doors proved to be pretty tricky as I was learning my carpentry skills as I went. Everything else on this property went relatively smoothly. It was competed in about two weeks and we had a tenant in place almost immediately. Note how simple things are when you buy turnkey rentals or almost turnkey rentals.

I was now back to working on the cat poop house and it was really starting to wear on me. I had been working 50-60 hour workweeks again, plus working on the houses every evening and weekend. Parham and I agreed that next time we would try and hire some things out, especially the painting as that probably wasn't the highest and best use of my time. This was the first time that I ever wondered if I would be able to do this. Could we really get to the point of financial independence before the work of the rentals became too much? To help alleviate the stress, I decided to contract out all of the plumbing work on the house. Unfortunately, this would prove to be a real headache, and not much of a stress reducer. One thing that you will learn is that you will go through many, many contractors before you find a good one. When you do find a good one, treat them like royalty.

We hired a plumber to install all of the new shower hardware, replace the hot water tank and connect a gas stove in the other house that we had just completed. The day that the plumber was supposed to show up and complete all of the work, we had an extreme cold event. Temperatures had dropped into the single digits and the plumber had received several calls concerning broken pipes, etc. They called that morning and asked if they could put off our job a couple days to help get there other (higher paying) customers back on-line. Not a problem at all I told them, however I needed the stove hooked up which should only take a couple minutes as the new tenant was moving in the next day. Our plumber had no issues with that and came by to take care of the stove before moving on to his other customers.

A few days later, I had to call them up to find out where we were on their schedule. Turns out they had forgotten to put us back on the schedule. When I did get them to show up, they disconnected the water heater and installed the shower fixtures. Why they didn't install the new water heater I don't know, but now they would have to make another trip out. When I got to the house to continue painting, my nose told me that they didn't leak test their work before they left. I had to have them back out the next day as the water heater gas line was leaking. They did promptly show up to cap the line the next day. Why would they cap the line and not install the new water heater which was sitting right there! If you are already there and the tank is already there why not? Clearly efficiency of time was not a big concern for them.

A couple of days later, they came back to install the new water heater, but turns out it was the wrong size and wouldn't fit. We would have to reschedule them, yet again, to install the water heater. Finally, the day came when they'd be installing the correct size water heater. Too bad they installed it in the wrong spot. The washer and dryer wouldn't fit back in their place with the new location of the hot water tank. I had to call them back and tell them the exact amount of space that needed to be left for the washer and dryer to fit. This seemed completely unnecessary as the washer and dryer were in the room. The dryer had simply been pulled out of the way to give them room to work. It wasn't like they couldn't have just pushed it into place when they were done. Either way, one additional trip for the plumber was in order.

This time when they were finished, I received a call to tell me they had left me exactly the amount of room that I had requested and that they were finished. That night when I went to the house to finish up the last few items, and I discovered that the dryer still would not fit. When the plumber had measured the space he left me, it was from the wall and he didn't account for the 0.5 inch width of the baseboard trim. I would've thought that after this many trips, he would've pushed the dryer four feet forward to make sure it fit before he left, but no that was just too much extra work.

Yet another phone call to the plumber. At this point the poor secretary was pretty exasperated with me. I explained to her that I told them how much space I needed and that this should not be very hard. I also told her that they had measured wrong and didn't take into account the baseboard. Finally, I mentioned to her that the dryer was right there so they could have made sure it fit before they left, but they hadn't. She scheduled another trip out to the house for the water heater. This time the water heater was installed in the correct spot (exactly where the old one had sat).

Only eight trips were required to get what was originally scheduled and bid as one day's work. I can't imagine that the plumber was going to make any money on this job. All of the work had been performed by the young son of the company's owner. Hopefully he learned that he should give his son more training before letting him loose with customers. In the end, it took over a month for the plumber to get everything installed and I am pretty sure that we were all very frustrated at that point. The bill for this job never showed up, and I just assumed it was the plumber's way of telling us sorry for all the issues. We would part ways and move on in life, no hard feelings.

Fast forward to just over a year later, we received a call from the secretary that we had never paid their bill and that they needed to get it paid. I asked her to please mail us the bill and we would gladly pay what we owed. I gave her our mailing address and again, the bill never showed up. I guess the attention to detail in their billing department was about the same as the attention to detail in their field work. Mr. Parker, if you are reading this, I will gladly remit payment as soon as we receive your bill.

I find that all too often when dealing with contractors, these are the kind of results we end up with. Finding a contractor that shows up on time, works without constant supervision and performs their work at a fair price is like finding a needle in a haystack. Finding contractors that can deliver consistently reliable performance is the holy grail of investing. Parham and I continued to struggle to find good contactors for years to come. As my friend, Gladimir, once told me, "you have to kiss some toads to find a prince." The only problem is it gets expensive kissing toads. Join an investors association, you will kiss fewer toads.

Now that the rehab was completed, we needed to find a tenant. Our properties in this neighborhood had yet to have a tenant move out and we decided to try to increase our price point on this property by $50 per month. This would make a decent upside to our projected profit margin on the property. We held an open house and received significant interest in the home. The tenants that we selected were a little unconventional, but it seemed to be a risk worth taking. Our new tenants were a younger couple in their mid-twenties and one of their brothers. This has turned out to be a very good situation, as the three get along well, take care of the property and have never been late on rent. When you split the $850 per month rent three ways, it gets to be very affordable. This group paid us more in rent than what we purchased the property for.

We received a significant amount of interest from Section 8 tenants when renting out this home. I have no problems with Section 8 tenants, and we have them in several properties that we own. However, there are lots of problems associated with people on Section 8 vouchers. You need to do a good bit of vetting when dealing with these tenants. Everyone has heard about the higher crime rates associated with Section 8 housing, but what was a shock to me was the fraud associated with the program. Over half of the Section 8 tenants that applied for the home openly informed me that they were defrauding the program when I told them about the income requirements. I have never seen so many people that were so comfortable with telling a complete stranger about how they were stealing from the taxpayers. This was an eye opening experience, which has repeated itself over and over. It is shocking how little effort the government puts in, to make sure our tax dollars end up in the right hands.

One lady told me about how Section 8 thought that her husband made $10.00 per hour but he actually made $12.00 per hour. Another lady told me about how Section 8 didn't know that her boyfriend was actually living with her and that he made good money so paying rent would not be an issue. The last one, which really took the cake, was a lady that told me paying the rent wouldn't be a problem as she planned to rent out the other bedroom to a friend. Section 8 wouldn't know about this income, and paying the rent wouldn't be an issue once her friend started paying her. I was aghast at what I had heard. Section 8 applicant after Section 8 applicant described the process of how to cheat the system perfectly. They seemed to know that there was little to no chance of getting caught or that if and when they do get caught they know Uncle Sam has no intentions of doing anything about the defrauding of the taxpayers.

I once had to evict a Section 8 tenant because she would not get rid of her pitbull. She lied on the application about having a pet, when confronted about having a pitbull she at first denied it was hers, then when she couldn't deny it anymore she stated that she would get rid of it. Getting rid of it simply meant chaining it to a post in the basement... We gave her a 30-day notice to vacate. She refused to leave or pay rent after that. We informed Section 8 about this and their answer was simply "this is a landlord issue". Well I thought getting evicted for non-payment of rent was a violation of the section 8 voucher program, apparently they were willing to overlook that violation. Material breaches of leases are also a violation of the program... They overlooked that too. Once we finally had a sheriff remove her from the property, Section 8 failed to pay us the rent they were escrowing on her behalf. Turns out Section 8 had allowed her to move into another apartment somewhere else 6 weeks earlier, and she told them that she had moved out of our place which she had not. We demanded that Section 8 honor their contract with us to pay their portion of the rent while she was in possession of the property. They informed me that they would not pay the rent as per our contract as they could not "double subsidize someone" and that they had already paid someone else for those months on her behalf... The fact that Section 8 was willing to violate a signed contract to assist someone who they were obligated to kick out of their system should tell you everything that you need to know about how government programs work. Ultimately, we did receive the payment that we were due, but we no longer accept any new Section 8 tenants. The juice isn't worth the squeeze.

Back to people defrauding the system, I want no part of defrauding the government, we run our business the right way. As a business owner, this is my livelihood and I am not risking it for someone that I don't know. Additionally, our properties are kept up to a very high standard. I don't need to cheat Uncle Sam in order to get tenants. If you do business the right way, you will never find yourself on the wrong end of something like this. You simply need to set high standards and leave those kinds of people and problems to the slumlords out there.

Believe me, there are plenty of slumlords in this business and they give us a terrible name. Before you go out there and become a slumlord, understand that being a slumlord is actually quite expensive in the long run. For each property that we have purchased, I have probably looked at 40 others that we didn't purchase. I see an awful lot of rental properties go up for sale that need tens of thousands of dollars' worth of work. These massive repairs are not always due to tenants tearing up these properties, it is due to landlords not performing basic and routine repair and maintenance. If those landlords were to put a minimal amount of money back into their properties, they would get better rents that would offset the costs of repairs, and the properties would either maintain or increase in value.

Slumlords cost themselves big time when they simply rent out properties, don't make repairs and then dump them on the market when they've become too big of a headache or when they become uninhabitable. They destroy the value of their asset by doing this, and instead of being able to sell their property at market value they receive pennies on the dollar when they sell. Plus, they lose their asset with this strategy. When your goal is to run a business into the ground, and you can't control when it hits the ground you are in trouble. What if you were banking on another years' worth of rent and the place just got to the point of no longer

being rentable? What if you still had a mortgage on the property?
Do yourself a favor and keep your properties in good shape and
rent to upstanding people. If you plan on buying more than one
property in a neighborhood, it is also good to make sure the
neighborhood stays nice. The last thing you need to do is bring
down the value of your other investments.

Chapter 15: The Grind Continues

Back at the mine, things were still pretty sketchy. We reduced our headcount by eliminating a managerial position and choosing not to fill open staff positions. This put added stress on everyone as this was the second staff reduction in two years. The amount of work had not changed, just the number of people doing the work. Amazingly enough, while our salaried staff was shrinking, our hourly staff was growing. This meant that there were now fewer supervisors overseeing more people. We were in the midst of a vicious cycle of productivity issues. As we reduced supervision, we lost productivity of our hourly work force. As the work force became less productive, we needed more hourly employees. More hourly employees translated to more cost reductions, which meant fewer salaried staff.

People can be just as short sighted in running a multi-billion dollar corporation as they can be when running a multi-thousand dollar rental property.

Another issue that we were struggling with was the need to update our equipment. We were trying to compete with companies that were using state of the art equipment, and we were running equipment that we had purchased used in the mid 70's. Outdated equipment and processes were probably our biggest obstacles to success. Even if our workforce was working at max productivity, the equipment wasn't able to take the workload. The manufacturers of some of our most critical equipment were no longer in business. The ones that were still around had cautioned us on numerous occasions that our equipment should have been retired years ago.

We brought one supplier in to look at our main ventilation fan. This fan is a critical piece of equipment that had been acting up for years, and we were afraid it was near the point catastrophic failure. In underground mining, you must continuously pump fresh air into the mine to keep the air fit to breath. We had about 75 diesel engines operating in our mine and these put a lot of exhaust fumes into the air. Without a constant supply of fresh air to remove the fumes from the mine, we would not be able to keep our workers safe. Another key problem with ventilation in underground mines is that in mining you use lots of explosives. After each blast, you must clear all of the blast fumes out of the mine before workers can reenter. The fumes from blasting can cause serious health effects from migraine headaches to death.

Our mine was ventilated using a single 800 horsepower fan that pumped about 300,000 cubic feet per minute of fresh air into the mine. Thus, we pulled out about 300,000 cubic feet per minute of contaminated air from the mine. This ensured that workers were always supplied with fresh air. The only problem was that our main (and only) fan was approaching 30 years old and was running on the original electric motor and all the original bearings. When the fan was new, it was state of the art with all sorts of sensors that would cause it to shut down if it detected that something was wrong. This way the fan would not continue to run and destroy itself if something went wrong. There was only one way to start the fan and there were 27 different sensors that could shut it down if one of them detected something amiss. Over the years, the sensors started detecting problems and instead of fixing the problems, we just disabled the sensors. We had done this to the point that all 27 sensors had now been removed from service. The only way that the fan would shut down now, was if the 800 horsepower electric motor got so hot that it melted and tripped the circuit breaker or if someone manually shut the power off to it. This was not a good situation.

We brought the manufacturer in to look at the fan and evaluate it. The person who was the lead engineer on the installation of the fan almost 30 years prior showed up for the inspection. He was now regional manager for the company. After his inspection of the fan, he told us that we needed to keep people away from it at all times, as it could catastrophically fail at any moment and he was not sure as to why it had not yet failed. He was absolutely certain that failure was imminent. I repeatedly asked how much longer we had before it failed, and most importantly how long would it take to get replacement parts when it did fail. Turns out the lead time on parts was about six months, and the fan was a one of a kind so there were no spare parts for it (except the ones we'd ordered 30 years earlier). Any parts that were not on site would have to be custom made.

After days of searching our warehouse for 30 year old parts, we packaged up all the spare parts we could find. Yes, we found almost all of them (except for the spare motor which we had lost, how do you lose a 4,000 pound 800 horsepower motor?) The parts had been stored directly on the salt floor in a long-forgotten part of our underground storage area. (When you run a salt mine, it is wise not to store high value metal parts on a pile of salt, placing them on shelves or in a surface warehouse may be a good idea.) We sent all the spare parts out for evaluation after 30 years of laying on a pile of salt. Lo and behold, 100% of the parts failed their evaluation and were deemed unusable. I can't imagine how storing precision-made parts on a pile of salt for 30 years could cause degradation. This was a perfectly bad situation that we found ourselves in, yet again.

Our group requested immediate funding to come up with a replacement option. Our Vice President denied the funding request almost immediately. It didn't meet our capital planning schedule... Our request for capital funding would need to be made at the appropriate time for funding in our *next* budget year. So as Engineering Manager I requested $500,000 in funding for a new fan for the next budget year. This was a complete crap shoot, as no one thought the fan would make it that long without complete failure. At this point, the best case scenario for funding of the new fan would involve funds being available in about 18 months. Between waiting on funds and the lead time on parts, this meant we were looking at 2 years before we'd have a new fan, something the mine would be closed without. We didn't have two years, and we knew it. So yet again, we were waiting for the next shoe to drop.

Fast forward a few months and kaboom, the motor on our fan failed. Without a spare, we were forced to shut down for a week while our procurement group searched for an outdated motor that we could buy that would fit. We found one for the low price of $75,000. Our director of mining flew in to yell at us about how he couldn't believe that we were going to lose a week of production over this and wanted answers as to why we didn't own a spare motor. He just, "had no idea how we could let ourselves get into this situation." This screw up had cost the company over half a million dollars in lost production and wages. I have never seen someone in such denial, he acted as if this was the first time in his life he had heard about our fan issues.

We got the motor replaced and reminded him of the project that we had put in to replace the fan. We also informed him that the problems with the fan still existed and we had not addressed those at all. With the motor problem solved, our director flew back to the corporate office. We didn't hear from him again until the following week, when we had to call and tell him that the fan had catastrophically failed and that it was irreparable. It wasn't like we could say, "I told you so," and hang up the phone. We had to sit there and listen to ultimatums about how we needed to have a plan in place on how to get things back up and running by the time he flew out. My only thoughts were "man I really didn't want to see that jackass again so soon, and I wonder if we could sell that week old $75,000 motor on ebay…"

This time we were lucky enough to have both the director and the vice president fly in to yell at us. Our vice president sat us down in a room and told us just how disappointed he was in our group. He could not believe that we had no back up plan. With something this critical it was just inexcusable not to have a spare. He went on to inform us that all of our other mines had dual fans so if one broke down the other would turn on and take over. That way there would never be a disruption of the mining activities. He wanted to know why we were not set up like this. Whose decision was it not to have dual fans? We needed accountability.

My first thought was to state that I had only been working at the mine for 2 years, and he had been the manager overseeing the mining operation in one capacity or another for over 20 years. Maybe we should be the ones asking the questions and him answering. The original fan installation was essentially designed and built 30 years prior to my birth! The current fan was 30 years old, almost my age. But somehow my group was responsible for the poor design and incompetent planning to deal with the easily foreseeable failure.

Matt, our maintenance manager, went ballistic after his ass chewing. He went on a rant of epic proportions about how he had personally been requesting a replacement for years and that funding to replace the fan was always denied. Furthermore, Matt was acutely aware that my group had requested funding for a new fan and that it was personally denied by the vice president himself. Matt had read and signed off on the funding request and knew it stated that, "the fan was at the point of imminent failure and that actions needed to be taken immediately." Now here he was, getting his ass chewed about not being prepared by the guy who had ensured that he was not prepared. This latest catastrophe ultimately led to loss of pay for all members of our senior management group, and the departure of one pissed off maintenance manager.

When it was all said and done, we had to purchase a new fan at a cost of approximately $500,000, plus we lost close to one month of production which equated to two million dollars of revenue. Worst yet, we lost credibility with our regulators and our employees. Our employees were convinced that as a management team we had no clue what we were doing. Our employees knew, just as we had known, that the fan had problems and we showed them exactly how not to be proactive. How, as a management team, could we hold them accountable for performance when we couldn't hold ourselves accountable to perform our most basic responsibilities? Once again, I was learning how NOT to do things: how NOT to run a company and how NOT to protect and value my credibility and integrity.

Chapter 16: The Real Estate Grind

It was all too familiar, life at the mine was getting more unstable by the minute. Even so, Parham and I continued our unrelenting drive to build our real estate portfolio. Using our frustrations with the mine as fuel, we purchased another property. We were now up to 10 rental properties. Our next couple of purchases convinced me of something I had long suspected about realtors: they are largely untrained and don't know anything about real estate. Many realtors don't even own their own homes! Full disclosure, I am/was a licensed realtor.

We went to see a HUD (foreclosure) home that was only ten years old and that was listed for $50,000. From the outside of the house, it was perfect. The only thing that I noticed was that the storage shed had been removed by the previous owners. Once the realtor opened the door, the issues became apparent. The walls were filled with holes, the house had been painted black at some point and the master bedroom was painted candy apple red, including the ceiling! The second bedroom was painted fluorescent orange. The vanities were missing from the bathrooms, all the appliances were gone, the kitchen sink had been removed and there were no doors on any of the closets. Curiously, everything had been removed in a professional manner as to not cause any underlying damage.

I knew a gold mine when I saw it, and we made a $45,000 offer that day. The house was ours, or so I thought. Unfortunately, our realtor was a complete flake. We had signed all of the forms, turned in the earnest money and received an email stating that our offer was accepted. We were informed of the closing company and were waiting for closing instructions. There should have been no issues at all. As the closing date approached,

I called the realtor concerned that we had not received anything yet from the title company. There had been no attempt to scam us into buying unnecessary insurance, no final amount to bring to closing, no location and time of closing, etc. Not a word from anyone.

I received an email back from our realtor the next day that everything was good. This really didn't answer my questions though, as I still didn't have any of the information that I needed. I called him back and left a message explaining to him what I needed. From that point forward, there was significant trouble getting a hold of him. I finally called the title company directly and was told that they didn't have any information about a closing for the property and that I should call my realtor. I called the bum several more times and received no answers.

Ultimately, I called up the title company and got the number to HUD, the organization selling the house. After about an hour on the phone with their automated systems, I got through to the human in charge of my property. The news was not good. The lady on the other end of the phone stated that they had canceled my contract to purchase the property as the realtor had never sent them the earnest money. How that could be? I had given him a cashier's check and had a copy of the check. The kind lady on the other end of the phone told me she had a copy of the check too. She went on to state that she can't cash a copy of a check.

My realtor had emailed them a copy of the check, and never contacted them again. They had never received the actual check and had emailed and called the realtor on many occasions and never received any response at all. The HUD lady even stated that they had gone so far as to send him an email stating that they were going to cancel the contract if he could not provide them with the actual earnest money check. My licensed realtor never responded to them!

So here I was, on the phone telling the HUD representative, "look, I gave him a check, I signed all of the paperwork, I've been proactively communicating my concerns with my realtor and had been told that everything was moving along just fine." The HUD rep could not believe this, so I sent her a copy of my emails to my realtor. That is when I really started to get some movement from HUD. They were sympathetic with my situation after I had convinced them that I was not some deadbeat investor that was just too lazy to get my paperwork and earnest money in. I was put through to a supervisor that told me that while my contract was canceled, they may be able to reinstate it, but I would need to get them the earnest money. This was a relief, though it was short lived. Turns out they had received and accepted another offer that morning, I would not be getting this house.

I was more than a little upset and could not believe that after all my efforts they could cancel my contract without ever informing me, the buyer, of the situation. Luckily, being stubborn is one of my best traits, and I was put through to yet another level of management where I spoke with someone that was going to go out of their way to help me. This lady managed to cancel the acceptance of the offer, as it had not been fully processed yet. She then reinstated my offer and told me I needed to get the earnest money to the title company that day. I left work at One O'clock and drove the one and a half hours to the title company and presented them with a cashier's check for the full purchase price. Problem solved, we were back on track to getting the property.

Now it was time for me to have a talk with my bum realtor's brokerage. I called and scheduled an appointment for the next day (Saturday) with the owner of the brokerage and went through the whole ordeal with her. She was very nice and seemed genuinely concerned about the gross negligence of one of her employees. I was adamant that this was not an acceptable situation and that my missing one thousand dollars of earnest money would be getting accounted for by the end of the day Monday. I wasn't sure exactly what licensing law had been broken, but I was fairly certain that when a licensed realtor takes a client's one thousand dollar check and disappears with it, that there is some sort of violation in there somewhere.

The broker was very professional, and as we were finishing up our conversation, she gave me a book titled "The Millionaire Real Estate Investor" which is one of the best investing books I have ever read. Eventually, everything got taken care of. My check was found and returned, I got the house, the lousy agent kept his job and I eventually placed my real estate license with that company. Funny how things work out.

Once we took ownership of the property, the real work began. I tried to do most of the work myself, but I was just so busy between work and the other houses that I had to hire a contractor to take on certain parts of the workload. This would be my first experience with hiring general contractors and I would learn a lot from it.

First of all, contractors love to make promises of doing a great job in a short amount of time at a competitive price. However, they are not exactly known for delivering on those promises. We received a fair quote on the price of painting the house and fixing the sheetrock. Remember, this house had previously been painted black with a candy apple red bedroom and a fluorescent orange bedroom. The painter we hired said that they would have the job finished in a week. One day to patch walls, one day to sand walls, one day to prime, and two days to paint. My painter had two helpers, one stopped showing up halfway through the project, and the other we nicknamed Braindead. Braindead seemed to be the lead man on the project, and he didn't have a clue what he was doing.

The project started off easy enough, I did the basic clean out of all the trash, old carpet, etc. I also installed the bi-fold doors that were all missing and replaced the downstairs ceiling fans as they were covered in funk. The fan blades had a coating of grease on them that was nearly impossible to get off, and worse yet there was so much lint and dust mixed into that grease it just made for an awful mess. Opting to replace the fans instead of clean them was definitely the right call. The walls in the kitchen area were covered in grease, and while I did my best to get that wiped down, it was a losing battle. After replacing the sink and all of the plumbing fixtures in the house, we were ready to paint. I called the painter and told him it was ready for him to take over.

This is where Braindead and his friend took over, and their "one-day job of patching" turned into a week. On day one, they started patching the walls like a normal human would do, but they only worked a half day due to the one guy needing to go see his girlfriend. On day two, they showed up late, and for some reason spent the day caulking around the trim and not patching the walls. On day three, they told me that the mud (joint compound) was not drying and they didn't know why. They had never had that happen before. Their boss showed up and turned on the heat which took care of the drying problem. On day four, they sanded the mud and had the walls prepared for the second coat of mud which went up on day five. On day six, the walls were given a last sanding and finally ready for paint. So much for patching being a "one day project."

Painting went fairly quickly downstairs, ceilings were done and walls had their first coat of paint on day one of painting. Curiously enough, the cabinets, which were painted black, had been avoided as that would be the hardest thing to paint. They were going to require oil-based paint and multiple coats of white paint to look good. At the start of day two, you could see all of the grease spots bleeding through the paint and appearing all over the kitchen walls. These walls needed to be primed in oil-based paint, but Braindead hadn't been able get any and it was clear that the grease stains on the wall were making short work of his craftmanship.

Around mid-week, I stopped by with their boss to help motivate them to speed things along. Their boss was a little upset at the lack of progress and had some words with them. This is when the first helper quit showing up. Guess he must have been sensitive, or was just scared of having to earn his pay. Either way, from here on out it was up to Braindead. His boss brought him a case of oil-based spray paint. This case of spray paint probably cost 5 times that of a gallon of regular oil-based paint, but hell it wasn't my money or my place to tell them how to do their jobs.

Braindead went to town spraying all of the grease spots with the spray paint, including the 2 foot by 15 foot backsplash in the kitchen. I don't know how long that took him, but a gallon of paint would have really saved time and cost. A nine inch roller can get an area like that done much more quickly. To make matters worse, he ran out of spray paint and wasn't able to get all of the touch ups done. After the oil-based spray paint had dried, he put another coat of paint over everything, even the areas that still needed oil-based primer. Yet again, more rework would have to be done when he came back to hit the missed grease spots. I probably should have fired the contractor at this point, as the owner obviously didn't care about training his employees or their onsite performance.

We were now well into our third week of painting, and I was getting a little annoyed at the time this was taking. My part of the project was nearly complete, and I could not get the carpet installed until the paint was done. At this point, my carpet installers had to be rescheduled which set me back on my timeline, and probably messed up their scheduling as well.

The upstairs was coming along well, except for the candy apple red ceiling. The ceiling was textured and apparently had never been primed or sealed. The candy apple red paint had never adhered and was peeling off in sheets. That evening, my wife and I took on the arduous task of peeling the paint off the ceiling. It sucked, but we tried to make it as entertaining as possible by holding a contest of who could pull off the biggest piece. She ended up with one piece that was about three feet long by two feet wide, the clear winner.

This paint peeling party amounted to one of our very rare date nights, the first in several years. We had hired a babysitter for the night and had intended on just stopping by to check on the project. When we got there, we both realized that if we didn't get the paint peeled off that ceiling Braindead was just going to paint right over it and create another mess. So, after our paint peeling date we got some fast food and headed home. Yes, owning rental properties means making sacrifices and this was just one of many. If you are not up for wasting an evening out doing something that you have paid someone good money to do, then this may not be the right business for you.

Nearing the end of week four, Braindead informed us that the project was finally complete. I thought the day would never come, and it hadn't. When I inspected the finished paint job, several walls had small cracks all throughout the paint. It looked like the paint had shattered. Turns out this was not an easy fix. Each time they had painted the walls, it came out like that. Braindead's boss brought in a paint specialist from Sherwin Williams to take a look. He figured it out immediately. The walls had very high moisture readings and it was affecting the drying of the paint. It is also why they had such a hard time getting the mud to dry.

The source of the moisture was the basement that had been flooded prior to us buying the home. Moisture from the basement had wicked up into the house and walls, causing our current problem. We had already pumped the basement dry, and luckily there were no mold issues, but it was the cause of these headaches. One automated basement sump pump and vent fan later, the problems would be gone forever. The paint problem could only be resolved by skim coating the walls priming and then another two coats of paint. Add another week to this "one week project".

At long last, the job was finished. My contractor called and wanted to be paid and I was more than happy to pay him. I was looking forward to parting ways after this project. We would chalk it up to a "one and done" interaction with this contractor and move on with life. Simple as that. I needed someone who could stick to a timeline and that could supervise their workforce. Better yet, I needed someone with a workforce. How do you call yourself a contractor when you only have one employee and it takes him over a month to do a simple job?

I scheduled a time to do a final walk through with the contractor and to make payment to him. When I met with the contractor to pay him, he wanted to discuss the payment. I didn't know what there was to discuss, but as I was already there with him, I guess we were going to discuss things. Cash? Check? Wooden nickels? I thought, "what does he need to discuss?" We had already agreed that he would be paid with a check from our business account and that I would be requiring a receipt. Turns out he wanted to discuss how much extra he should be paid due to all of the delays and cost overruns associated with the greasy walls and the high moisture.

At the mention of this, I was prepared to discuss how much less he should be paid due to all the delays. I figured my holding costs on the house were about $25 per day, and since they were four weeks behind he owed me a $750 discount. I also argued that this amount didn't even include the delay that I would be incurring on getting the carpeting done as I was now off the carpet company's schedule.

The discussion did not go very well, we were both upset that the other guy was trying to screw us. I felt very justified sticking with our contract, and my position was that he bid on the job against other contractors. Those other contractors surely saw the grease all over the walls and took that into consideration in their quotes. If he didn't take that into consideration in his quote, then shame on him and next time he would know better. As for the high moisture, no one could have expected that, but as a professional contractor he should have been able to identify the problem prior to painting the same wall four separate times. I figure the loss I took on him missing the deadline was probably equal to or less than the loss he took on the moisture issues.

This contractor, by the way, was not exactly the lowest bid. I had one bid $200 below his and one bid that was $100 above his. In the end, we parted ways and have never done business together since. Get use to situations like this, I have. It occurs way more than it should with contractors.

Another big takeaway from this project was that I needed to be very careful when preparing my scope of work. Your scope of work needs to detail exactly what materials are to be used, specify the required completion date as well as penalties for missing that date, and the expected level of craftsmanship. This particular contractor had used some very cheap paints, which can sometimes wipe right off of walls as they're being washed. The difference between good paint and cheap paint is about 5 bucks per gallon. If you can't afford that, then you are in the wrong business. We now specify exactly what paint will be used in our properties, and in most cases, supply the paint. In this industry, you tend to learn your lessons the hard way, and this was no exception. I have also found that many contractors balk at the idea of severe penalties for missing deadlines. See, they almost always miss their deadlines and don't want to be held accountable. I try to take the edge off by putting bonuses into our contracts for beating the deadlines. Think about it, if I give them a $50 per day bonus for beating the deadline, my rehab gets done faster and my tenant is in place sooner, meaning an incentive payout to a contractor doesn't cost me a dime. If we assume carrying costs are $25 per day, and profit is $15 per day (once a tenant is in place), this means that the $50 per day bonus that I am paying really only costs me about $10 per day. I would gladly hand a contractor $70 to finish a job a week early versus having a rehab drag on for an additional week. Time is money, and this is one of the cheapest ways you will ever find to "buy" time.

Chapter 17: Supply and Demand

We did not wait long after completing that project before we started out on another, our eleventh property and newest addition was a real gem. It needed very little work, had waterfront views of Lake Erie and was within one hundred and fifty feet of a park. An investors dream, it would always be rented as its location was perfect. I thought the only issue would be that the demand for one-bedroom houses is pretty low. Additionally, the detached garage had been converted into a bar, complete with dart lanes and a big screen TV. Looking back at it, I can't believe just how bad my assumption was that there would be no demand for a one-bedroom house. We now own several one-bedroom houses and have learned that there is incredible demand for them.

Think about it, half of all marriages end in divorce. That's a lot of people paying child support, alimony, etc. There are also many people living alone that don't need a ton of space. These are great candidates for smaller homes. Additionally, there are an absolute ton of baby boomers that have never bothered to save a dime and are now trying to make it on Social Security. Those Boomers can't pay a lot, but are great and quiet tenants. Just think for a minute, the market for smaller homes fits so many different demographics. These are basically standalone apartments, that are great for someone on an apartment budget who just wants a little space to call their own.

One-bedroom houses are like hens' teeth, there aren't many around and they are illegal to build under current codes. This makes them very rare, and therefore valuable. What do you get when you have a fixed (or slowly decreasing) supply and increasing demand? One hell of a deal if you're on the supply side. My one-bedroom homes are incredibly profitable.

The best part of the equation is the arrogance and prejudice of most investors. I can't tell you how many investors turn their noses up at this type of property. Most investors want a three-bedroom house with either one or two baths because they are easy to resell, or they can see themselves living in a house like that. They look at what they want, not what the market wants.

These investors have to bid against owner occupants to buy these houses. Owner occupants will pay more for houses every time, as they are buying with emotion. Investors should be buying based on numbers, not emotions. When you are competing with people buying with emotion, you are in the wrong market my friend. I am not complaining, because I don't want these "investors" in my market. I am glad to let them overpay for properties and go broke, or best case scenario just not make a good enough return to justify staying in the game. I will keep seeking out and buying the houses that no one wants. The one- and two-bedroom houses are rentals through and through. If you are buying for the long term, why would you care about resell value? One- and two-bedroom houses trade like commodities, commodities that no one wants. These ugly ducklings sell for what they are worth on the rental market or below. That's it! Banks price them off of returns, investors selling them price them based on returns, we buy them based on returns. It's easy, and I like easy, easy makes money. Lot's of it.

Going back to my one-bedroom house, I again learned the hard way just how bad real estate agents can be. You must be careful when dealing with real estate agents, they're often untrained and not entirely professional. This would be yet another purchase where we did business with a shady real estate agent. Just a preface and reminder before I get started on this story: I am/was a licensed agent, not all real estate agents stink, just most of them.

Prior to even purchasing this property, problems started. The owners had done significant remodeling and were 99% finished but there were a couple of things that needed to be done prior to us making the purchase. First, they had converted the garage into a bar. They had built a very nice tiled bar, but they had about 15 pieces of one inch by two inch decorative tile that still needed to be installed. I figured this was a pretty easy task for them to complete. Also, they had started to install stacked stone on the chimney and never finished. There were two pallets of the stone in the back yard. I had placed in the contract that the stone would be left so that we could finish this project. The day before closing, we did our final walk through, and the tile had been installed with painter's caulk instead of mastic. The work was very sloppy, with caulk everywhere and the tiles at odd angles. I informed our agent that we would be taking a $500 deduction off of the price of the house for the poor quality of the work, and explained that we expected the work to be redone correctly this time. Additionally, I informed her that we noticed that the two pallets of stone were gone, and we required that they be returned as the contract stated. I was less than impressed with the seller's behavior.

I quickly received a call that the sellers would not agree to a $500 deduction, but would return the stone. I told her that was not a problem at all, and that I completely understood. I just wanted her to inform the sellers that the deal was off, and we were done. I requested that she complete the mutual release forms effectively ending the deal. I wasn't going to play games.

Quite a while later, the realtor informed me that the sellers had agreed to both return the stone and give a $500 deduction. I was Glad the sellers had a change of heart and decided to abide by the terms of our contract, because I really liked the house and thought it would be very profitable.

I thought that I had made my position very clear and that the sellers understood, the terms of the original contract were to be enforced. I mean the realtor called me to tell me they would abide by the contract and give the $500 deduction. On my way to closing the following day, I stopped by the house to do another final walkthrough, to make sure the stone was returned and that nothing out of line had occurred. I clearly didn't trust these people. Guess what? Only one pallet of stone had been returned. I called the realtor again and informed her that there would be another $500 deduction in the price of the house due to the missing pallet of stone. To be honest, I probably didn't need both pallets to finish the job, but it was a matter of principle. These people just didn't want to do what they said they would do. Besides, if anyone was to sell back the stone it was going to be me, as I had negotiated it into the purchase. The realtor was not very pleased with me after this call, but I told her I had a cashier's check in my hand to purchase the property in cash and that I would stop and get myself lunch on the way to closing. This would give her about 30 minutes to get the deduction written up, signed and over to the title company. Otherwise the deal was off, I wasn't playing games with these people. Amazingly enough, she managed to get it done. There was $1,000 taken off the price of a $50,000 house solely because the sellers were not ethical and didn't want to perform as agreed.

Don't you worry, they got me back. Their unethical behavior didn't end with a couple of pallets of stone and shoddy work. As I was pulling out of the parking lot from closing on the house, I received a call from the realtor. She proceeded to tell me that there was a "suspected" water main leak under the house that I should check out. I still can't believe that I didn't sue her, the seller, and the title company over this. The leak was obviously known about as the title company had to clear the previous two months of water bills, which exceeded $1,500, that had not been

104

paid. When we did our walk through of the house, the water was on and everything appeared to be working. When we did our inspection, the water was off but I didn't really think twice about it as everything else looked to be in good shape. The tenants had already moved out, and we figured that they had just turned it off for that reason. Take away: make sure all utilities are on when performing your inspections. The water main leak was under the house and simply flowing straight to a drain, so there was no evidence of the leak.

Fixing the broken water line proved to be one of my more challenging tasks. The water main came in somewhere under the kitchen floor, which was tiled. The house had a concrete pad poured around three sides of it, so there was no access underneath the house except from the back yard (about 15 feet from the kitchen area). I didn't mention that this house was originally built as a summer cottage and it was literally less than 6 inches off of the ground. Yes, that is correct, the only way to get to the broken pipe was to either tear up the tile floors or tunnel my way in from the back of the house. Being a miner, I went with the tunneling option.

It was a miserable, cold, wet and dirty job. I had to lay on my stomach and use a garden trowel to dig out the ground in front of me. I would shovel this into a small bathroom trash can that I kept in front of me as well. Once the trash can was filled I would then army crawl my way backwards out from under the house, so that I could dump the dirt out and go at it again. Eventually four truckloads of dirt would be removed, one small bathroom trash can at a time.

When I did find the broken pipe, it took me less than ten minutes to fix it. Three days of digging for ten minutes of fixing. Yep, can't believe I didn't sue them over that (I have never sued anyone other than tenants that didn't pay rent). Unbelievably, I didn't even leave the realtor a poor review on social media or anything. That said, I have never again done business with that brokerage and never will. What goes around comes around, the brokerage no longer exists as a result of its parent company having to pay massive fines for defrauding customers. Back to that whole running your business with integrity thing, it starts at the top, lack of integrity at the top spreads like a poison through the whole organization.

Chapter 18: Insurance Companies

Staying on the topic of questionable integrity, it was around this time that one of our homes in Virginia was vandalized. Our tenants of 5½ years had ran into marital issues. The wife came home one day and told her husband that she wanted a divorce and would be moving out the following week. He didn't take the news well, and somehow all the water pipes in the house got ripped out of the walls, flooding the house and conveniently destroying all of her belongings.

Amazingly, the local keystone cops were unable to solve this "who done it" mystery. Their inability to solve the mystery was undoubtedly tied to the amount of time they dedicated towards investigating. The investigation was initiated and completed the same afternoon, with no findings of fault. One would think that a $40,000 vandalism would garner some attention, but it didn't. The police often get a bad rap, but this time they really deserved it. This is what happens when you get very, very, small municipalities running their own police departments. They simply don't have the capabilities to perform the jobs they are tasked with performing. That city is just lucky that no real crime ever happens there.

Once the insurance part rolled around, the real problems began. Tourists, our insurance company, did everything possible not to pay the claim. Tourists spends millions on training, and our claims representative was undoubtably trained in their process. ~~Too bad their process was designed to minimize payouts and not make their clients whole.~~ Sorry lawyers say I can't write that. Apparently, it was simply just an unfortunate human error that the claims representative measured every room short when calculating square footage of damaged flooring, and it was yet another unfortunate human error that he incorrectly counted the number of steps on the staircase when calculating how many to repair. The unfortunate human errors continued when he measured the square footage of every wall needing repair incorrectly. It was just a profound coincidence that all of these mistakes happened on the same insurance claim. I mean, what are the chances that a highly trained representative would get every measurement wrong and in the insurance company's favor?

After many hours of arguing on the phone with Tourists, a supervisor was assigned to assist me with my claim. This person was a real winner. He managed to get the square footage calculations corrected. I really couldn't lose that argument, right? However, he seemed to think that the damage in the bedrooms was separate from the damage in the rest of the house. After many hours of back and forth, he agreed to pay but only as a separate claim requiring a separate deductible. He wanted to charge each room that was vandalized as a separate incident because they did not appear to be damaged in the same event. As far as I was concerned, it was one event, but he didn't agree. I lost this battle, but let them know exactly how I felt about them. If my memory serves me correctly, a settlement of $17,000 was offered. I thought this to be laughable and told them as much.

Tourists proceeded to tell me that I could take the check, or repair the property to exactly as it was prior to the incident and they would pay for the cost of repairs. I only had a budget of around twenty thousand dollars as that was the amount of damage before they took depreciation into account. I told them there was no way that I could get the place fixed for $20,000. My new claims representative told me I could. I told him I couldn't and if they thought they could, then they could go for it and call me when it was done.

At this point, Tourists stopped paying for the loss of rent as their representative had only authorized this coverage for two months. They had allocated only two months for the entire repair process. Here we were, two months in and we hadn't even agreed on a repair price or found a contractor willing to take on the job for what they determined the repair cost to be. We did eventually get the loss of rent payments taken care of. Just another headache in the process and an unfortunate human error in estimation of the time it would take to repair the property. Finally, Tourists recommended a contractor to us who had worked with Tourists in the past and had agreed to take on the job at their budget.

We were off and running on the repairs, thank goodness. After the numerous change orders that their contractor put in due to problems with the original repair estimate, the final repair price came in at $45,000.

Looking back, it still makes me mad. I wanted to spend some extra money on making the master bathroom a little nicer and going a little lower end on some of the other items, but since they failed to make a reasonable offer, we ended up with the work their contractor did. He did a decent job, but did I really need brand new solid hardwood cabinets in a $90,000 house? Sure would have been nice to have regular cabinets and a master bath with something other than a bottom of the line Home Depot corner shower enclosure. Better yet, I would have taken $35,000 cash and sold the house to a local investor, and we all would have been better off. All they had to do was make me a fair offer to begin with.

Big takeaway form this incident: make your tenants carry renter's insurance. When your renters carry renter's insurance, it means their insurance company is on the hook, and you are in a much better place in the negotiations. I got to keep the house a few more years, and suffered many more headaches in the process.

Once the repairs were made, we hired a property management company to deal with this property. That was yet another fiasco. The house that years ago I thought would be a gold mine was turning into a profound money pit and headache.

The property management company we hired found a tenant, put them in place and promptly sent us a repair bill on the house for $2,000. When I called to find out what the repair bill was for, they informed me that when water was turned on to the house, the dining room ceiling and fan were damaged along with a wall as there was a water leak. Turns out the company that did the repairs for the insurance company put a nail through one of the new water lines that they had ran, and since the property management company hadn't notified us of the problem until after the fact, I couldn't go back to the general contractor and have them perform the repair under warranty. I would eat this $2,000. Now that I had just taken another $2,000 loss on this property, we immediately informed the property management company that they were not to perform work on the property ever again without our permission. I believe that our contract with them limited them to only performing repairs under $500 without prior consent anyways…

About 6 months later, I received a call from the tenant. Yes, I the owner received a call from the tenant. This is not supposed to happen when you are paying someone to manage both the property and the tenant. The tenant was upset that the damage to the ceiling had not been fixed from the water incident when she moved in. I was very nice to her and let her know it would be fixed promptly.

I was not so nice to the property management company. How had they not finished the repair? I'd paid $2,000, and the job wasn't finished? The repair only involved replacing the fan and sheetrock, as well as fixing a hole in some PEX tubing.

Unbelievable. So, another check was written to finish repairing the ceiling damage. Several calls were made about my expectations of them as a management company, and what my definition of management was. Another six months and several more issues with the property management company later, we reached the breaking point. I received a call that the built-in window unit air conditioner was broken and that there was a broken outlet as well. The management company wanted to bring in an electrician to look at the outlet and they wanted $300 for a new window unit. They didn't know how much it would be to install the window unit, but they charged $45 per hour and required two people to perform the change out. I always try to be professional, but sometimes I fail. This time I failed. I asked them what was wrong with the A/C unit, and pointed out that it had just been replaced during the insurance repairs. They didn't know what was wrong with it, other than it was making a loud noise and since window units are not repairable, they needed to replace it.

As for the outlet, I wanted to know what it was doing. Apparently, it was tripping out all the time. I asked the property manager when was it tripping out and what was the tenant doing when it tripped? He didn't know anything as he hadn't been to the house, nor had he asked the tenant any further questions. I instructed him to go to the house and find out what was going on. Our property manager called me the next day with good news! Turns out it was a sheet of paper that had fallen into the fan housing of the window unit that was causing the noise. Removing the paper fixed that problem. As for the outlet, it was tripping when she was using the microwave. The microwave, toaster oven and a couple of other items were all on the same breaker. I didn't need to hire an electrician to figure this one out, and neither did they.

We parted ways soon after that. Our property managers wanted to spend a significant amount of my money on repairs that were all completely unnecessary due to their inability to go look at the house they were managing. Beware, this experience is par for the course as far as property managers go. After all, they are just real estate agents in the end, and you know my thoughts on that group. In my state, all that is required for a real estate license is 4 weeks of training and a two year degree. You also have to pass a test, but if you can spell your name you can pretty much pass the test.

Chapter 19: Getting help

We can only get so far on our own, and at this point in my investing career we had made several mistakes as already noted. These are fun stories to tell now, but they were not very fun at the time, and many could have been prevented with better knowledge and planning. My wife and I joined our local real estate investors association, the Great Lakes Real Estate Investors Association, in the fall of 2013. It was here that I would meet Gary Pallini, who ran the organization. At my third meeting, I was talking with Gary and he told me that I should be able to quit my job and become a full-time real estate investor in only 12 months. Well, Gary was wrong, or perhaps he was right, and I just didn't listen to the instructions very well.

Either way, I cannot complain as I became a full-time real estate investor a little less than 36 months after that conversation. Gary has become quite a friend and mentor over the last couple years, and there is no way that my wife and I would be able to do the things that we do without the help and advice that I receive by being a member of the Great Lakes REIA. REIA's are nationwide, which means there is one in just about every community. Go find one near you and join! Be careful though, not all of these organizations are the same. Here in Cleveland, Ohio we have four. Only one focuses solely on education and that is what you need, an education. Education tends to decrease the tuition that you pay to the School of Hard Knocks. I attend every single meeting. It doesn't matter what is going on, it doesn't matter how much it is snowing, I make time and you should too. If you have any desire to succeed in this business, you need an education. It will save you a fortune on avoidable mistakes and help you discover tactics that will give you a competitive edge.

Regardless of industry, education is the key to competing with and eventually outperforming your competition. One way we outperform our competitors is by beating them in key metrics. Taxes paid as a percentage of revenue is a metric that I use to help judge not only risk but how well I am doing overall. Here in northeast Ohio, tax rates are sky high. We maintain a competitive edge by owning properties with favorable tax positions. If you own a home that is being taxed at $500 less than every other home in the neighborhood, then you have some options. For example, you can pay more for the house to win a bidding war, keep rents lower to help occupancy rates or you can continue to run your property exactly like everyone else on the street and make $500 more than them. Whatever you choose, you need an education to help you become sophisticated enough to find and maintain properties in these types of market positions. As a side note, I do not recommend paying more to win a bidding war, I try to be a buyer of last resort, and therefore I very, very, rarely increase a bid due to competition.

Another area where education is key is in material selection. Everyone seems to want to put in higher end appliances, or high-end counter tops in an effort to bring in premium rents. The reality is that some of those products don't stand up well to tenants. In my opinion, durability is the name of the game. You don't need to listen to me though, go to your local investors association and pay attention to the vendors that sell products into this segment of the industry. Those vendors will tell you what people are buying and what products are performing in the market. They will also guide you away from products that you will regret, because if you regret buying a product you probably won't buy again from that vendor. Vendors like repeat business, they are not very likely to steer you in the wrong direction. Last but certainly not least, the single most important reason you should attend investor meetings is to be around other investors. You are the average of the people that you associate with. Associate with investors and you will become one, associate with lazy people and you too will become lazy.

I try and make the most of our networking sessions and have learned so much from talking to other investors. Hearing their war stories is invaluable and offers perspective when things aren't going the way that you envisioned. Remember, it can always be worse and there is probably someone else in the room that has seen and experienced something worse than what you are going through. If they can make it through, so can you.

One day I mentioned to Gary how much money we had dumped into our first house and how we'd ended up having to sell it for less than we purchased it for. Due to our expenses and the housing bubble, we lost about $40,000 on it. That area never recovered, and 15 years after the bubble burst prices were still below 2006 levels. Gary told me, "well your first real estate lesson/purchase came cheap." His first venture in real estate apparently cost him $72,000. Amazingly, neither of us gave up we stuck to it and figured out a way not to let that happen again. Being a member of an investor group, you will be able to be around those people who haven't given up despite all of their trials and tribulations.

I can't tell you the countless number of people that I have met at the investor association that don't make it. They come to three, four, perhaps five meetings, and then you never see them again. I find it somewhat humorous, most of these people have fancy business cards that often state they are the president of their company, or even the CEO. These are the people that are there to get rich quick. Once they figure out that work is involved they stop showing up.

If you think investing is a way to get rich quick, you are absolutely foolhardy and you are wasting your time and money. Outside of my family, the two things I am most protective of are time and money, specifically my time and money. Emphasis on time. Getting rich doesn't happen overnight, and it surely doesn't involve business cards and logos. My wife and I didn't find the time or money to spend on those things until our company's 5th year. My wife and I have been very successful in our real estate investing business and we are far from rich. We do this full-time and still have not splurged on any big purchases. We are committed to the long game and that means continuing to grow the business. While we may not consider ourselves to be rich, we do consider ourselves to be wealthy. There is a difference, a big difference. Rich people are not always wealthy, in fact most rich people are not wealthy.

Being rich just means that you have a lot of money to spend and that you don't have to worry about how you spend it. Rich is simply having a high level of discretionary spending. People that don't think about how they spend their money don't often become wealthy because they don't do the things necessary to develop wealth. They just don't save or invest. We do very well, and we never have money to waste. We put virtually all of our money back into building our business and creating wealth. Being wealthy means you don't have to worry about going to work to be able to afford to live. That is my goal. I would much rather not work than drive a fancy car or live in a fancy house.

I once had a lady that worked for me who was rich. Her salary was considerably less than mine, but she had a lifestyle many times that of mine. She changed cars every few years and only leased high end vehicles. She wore designer clothes, she and her husband custom built a $385K house. She would brag about how often she flew, and took great pride in being able to travel to destinations that many of us hadn't been to, and couldn't imagine going to. Did I mention that she was 32 years old? Great for her to be able to afford all of that, but she had no wealth at all. She will be rich all of her life, however I believe she will work well into her 60's and never have real wealth.

One day she was in the office practically in tears as she found out that she owed the IRS ~$10,000. She didn't know how she was going to be able to afford to pay the bill. If she had created an emergency fund or put money into savings, she would not have had a problem. Instead, she had a big problem, she had no wealth at all, her only source of money was her paycheck, and most of it was spoken for. What wasn't spoken for went to fancy clothes and dinners. None of that paycheck went to a savings account. People who have the income level that she and her husband had should not find themselves in a position where they can't pay their bills, but here she was. She was rich and she never worried about spending money. I'd hoped that this situation would have taught her something about planning and personal finance, but unfortunately, I don't think it did. Most people of that mindset never learn that the way to become wealthy isn't by making a million dollars, it's by not spending a million dollars. The book Millionaire Next Door is a great read and talks about this quite a bit.

Chapter 20: Overloaded

Going back to my work life balance, it was becoming clear that we needed to find me another job. We could not continue to grow the business the way that we had been, and still have me working the long hours I had been working. We had made offers on several properties that had all been accepted, and I was staring at a massive set of projects coming down the pike that I knew I would not be able to handle. We had made offers on a duplex and three single-family homes, all within a two month span. All of the properties were at incredible prices, which I believe reflected the bottom of the market. I've not seen such high quality homes on the market at such how prices since that time. I couldn't afford to pass up the opportunities in front of me. We leveraged everything to make these purchases. I took a $50,000 401(k) loan, bank loans and we even took a private loan. We made it happen, but we also needed to find a way for all these repairs to be done by someone other than myself. Additionally, we needed to get these things cash flowing quickly. I hate having properties sit empty, we needed them rented and we needed the cash. We needed the cash to fund the repairs, we were on fumes but could see the light at the end of the tunnel.

We hired a contractor that was a member of our REIA group. He had not been a member long, however he seemed better than most. I had the contractor come out to quote on the first property that we were scheduled to close on in this round of purchasing. The quote and timeframe were very competitive, but looking back at it I should've seen red flags from the beginning.

First, I had made certain to put the materials to be used in writing. I had learned this lesson before and wasn't going to have an issue related to improper use of materials again. Turns out they didn't read the contract very well, and they used paint that wasn't in the specs. I was annoyed, but did not make them repaint the house. It was close enough to the right color, just not the right brand. I wanted something that I could duplicate. If walls needed to be touched up in the future, I need to be able to match the paint exactly and now I was in a position where I couldn't. To make things worse, they had diluted the paint slightly to put it through their spray guns and it had a slight affect on the color. This meant that even what they touched up by hand didn't match perfectly, and I would never be able to match it later. What a pain!

Another red flag that I should have noticed was that the supervisor never showed up to the project site one single time. The job got done and it was done well, but there was no supervision and this would cause problems in the future. I was happy enough with the work that I used them again on the next house. They did a good job there, but I cut the paint part out of their contract and painted it myself. Again, no major complaints on the second job but the quality of work had dropped a little, and while this job was smaller than the last one, it took longer to complete. The last of my spring shopping spree was near closing, and so far we had made the timing work for both units of the duplex and one of the single-family houses.

We were now ready to move on to the first major project. It was a big project mainly due to the size of the house. This property was a large single-family home with a full basement and a finished attic that had been converted to a master bedroom. Turns out the complexity of this project would be impacted because it was located in a municipality that we had not done business in before. Note to reader, know the municipality you are working in and how they operate. I didn't talk to my fellow investors about this municipality, and I should have. It is the only property we have ever purchased there, never again.

We initially weren't concerned about the municipality, because we were not going to do anything that required a permit. The project started off on time with the crew showing up and immediately starting on pressure washing and repainting of the garage. We typically start the outside work first to give our properties curb appeal. Our new neighbor immediately called the police department about the contractor who was pressure washing the garage. Apparently, he was concerned that the contractor was using the other neighbor's spicket to feed the pressure washer. The police didn't seem to care, especially since the contractor had asked permission. However, they did call the building department to let them know that there was a contractor at a house doing work without a permit. Really, is it the job of the police to report people pressure washing houses? I mean don't they have better things to do?

This led to the building inspector calling me up on our first vacation in years and asking what we were doing and why we didn't have a permit. I was in Chicago getting ready to board a plane, so I politely explained to the inspector that I didn't have much time. He took this as an invitation to restart the Spanish Inquisition. I told them that what we were doing was a pretty simple renovation. We were repainting the shed and the inside of the house, changing light fixtures and replacing some old paneling with sheetrock in one room. I told the gentleman that I was pretty sure we didn't need a permit for any of that, and he seemed to agree. Well, when my plane landed I had a voicemail from the contractor that they had received a stop work order. Really, what the hell?

The contractor was very upset with me and wanted to know why I didn't give them a heads up that the inspector was coming. I told him I didn't know that he was coming and that it shouldn't matter anyways as we were not doing anything wrong. Well, the inspector thought otherwise.

It turns out that my contractor had lied to the inspector. When the inspector showed up, they told him they were just helping a friend and were not contractors. Yes, that is what they actually told the inspector. Meanwhile, I had already told the inspector the truth of what we were doing so he was wise to their line of crap. It really didn't matter what I had told him, as I am sure a house owned by an LLC is pretty obviously not being repaired by "friends of the owner" at noon on a Wednesday.

The inspector proceeded to throw the book at them, and me in a round about way. He wrote them up for working without a permit, failing to register as a contractor in the city, etc. That last one carried a pretty big fine, plus a registration fee. My contractor would be delayed over two weeks and lost about $1,000 in fees and fines. They required him to get an electrical permit for changing the light fixtures, then he had to use a licensed electrician to actually change out the fixtures. Needless to say, he would be losing money on this job as the contract was for less than $5,000. Fortunately for me, my contract clearly stated that the contractor was responsible for all permits. I had to point this out to him later when he wanted to bill me for the fees and fines he had accrued. He would not have needed permits if his employees had not lied to the building inspector. Again, going back to honesty and integrity. If they would have been open and honest with the inspector, I bet they would have been completely fine. The city just would have made him pay a registration fee and been on his way, but his employees had to lie to them. By the way you don't need a permit to change a light fixture, but do you really want to fight that in court?

During the delay associated with getting the permits, we started on the other house that we had just closed on. We used the

121

same contractor, this way I kept his crews busy during the idle time. This time my contractor didn't even come out to bid on the project, he just had the crew go straight to the house and provide him an estimate which he wrote up and sent over to me to be signed. Guess this was another red flag that I ignored. This new project required adding a wall to create a third bedroom, replacing lots of blown plumbing lines, installing all new kitchen cabinets, adding a dishwasher and redoing the bathroom. They claimed they would get this done in the two weeks they were delayed on the other house. Meanwhile, my work really blew up on me during this time and I didn't stop by the house once during this two week period. Big mistake. When it is your project, you need to be there, I wasn't there, and I was about to incur the consequences.

I received a call from the owner of the contracting company asking to be paid as they had finished the work at the second house. They would now be starting back on the previous house since they now had the stop work order lifted. So, imagine my surprise when I stopped by to inspect the final product, and it was horrendous. The wall they added went right through a return air vent. To make matters worse, the vent was actually out of service, so they could have just removed it and sheet-rocked it over, but instead they proceeded to stuff it full of trash. To this day I wonder what must have been going through their minds. So again, the obvious solution of sheet-rocking over the hole didn't come to mind. Instead, they cut the metal vent in half and reattached it on either side of the new wall that intersected it. So now the vent was half over sheetrock, and half over a hole stuffed with trash on both sides of the new wall. If they thought the vent was functional then why would they stuff trash in it? If they knew that it was out of service then why not sheetrock over it??? The kitchen looked good except they forgot to plumb in the new dishwasher, and the bathroom was a complete disaster.

The clowns put the new sheet rock around the tub, but used the wrong kind (not green board) and wrong size (quarter inch instead of 3/8th inch). This resulted in the tub surround not matching up to the tub correctly, and they addressed this by simply cutting an additional 3 inch piece of quarter inch sheetrock and placing it all the way around the bottom of the tub. Next, they glued the surround over their new creation. When it was all said and done, it looked like a ski ramp right at the bottom of the shower surround. To top it off, the surround was bubbled very badly and had already starting to come off of the wall. The surround had been adhered with painter's caulk and not liquid nails or a real adhesive.

The last part of the job involved them replacing the sewer gas stack pipe that was cracked. They did a good job replacing the pipe from the crawl space to the ceiling of the main level, but they fell short on knowing how to tie the new plastic pipe back into the old cast iron pipe. (Helpful hint: you can buy a rubber coupling for this at Home Depot for about $10). The solution they came up with was to increase the pipe diameter from 4 inches to 6 inches and sleeve it over the cast iron. Unfortunately, this didn't pass the smell test. The bathroom smelled of the fumes that they were venting into it due to their repair. How could they not seal the pipe? I was dumbfounded as this was the same crew that had already done quite a bit of work for us and I'd come to know their craftsmanship as not great but at least acceptable. This looked like they suddenly forgot how to do basic construction work. I called up the contractor and asked if he had checked on his crew at all in the past two weeks. Of course, he hadn't.

We had a good conversation about how I would love to pay him, but the work wasn't passable and would need to be addressed in order for him to get paid. He stated that they would start back on the other house, and he would come out late the following week to see what needed to be addressed. We all make mistakes, and letting that crew set foot on one of my properties again was one that I made. They started back on the "permit" house, replacing the paneling with sheetrock. To save money and time, or maybe just because they didn't give a shit, they hung all the new sheetrock using exactly 4 nails per sheet. One nail in each corner of a 4 foot by 8 foot piece of sheetrock. For those of you who don't know much about this process, screws are supposed to be used and there should be around 20 screws holding every sheet in place. Again, if I had been at my jobsite, I would have known what was going on. My problem was that I was stuck working my butt off at my 9-5 job. Truly, this job had changed into more of a 7-7 those days. Finally, I met up with the contractor to show him the work at the house that they claimed was finished.

He was mortified when he saw the work, however he still had the audacity to inform me that it would cost extra to plumb in the dishwasher as that wasn't in the original quote. What do you mean it wasn't in the quote? They installed the new cabinets, and the new dishwasher. Who puts "install new cabinets" and "install dishwasher" on a quote not expecting it to be functional once the job was completed? We left that job, and he said that the crew would be there the next day to fix their mistakes.

They showed up the next day, and while they did plumb in the dishwasher, they also stuffed rags in the space where the new stack pipe went over the old one to seal it up. Additionally, they used what appeared to be an entire tube of window caulking to re-adhere the tub surround, and they decided to seal the vents they had cut in half by taping black garbage bags over the back of them.

It was then that I received another invoice in my email asking me to pay for the now completed job. I called the contractor and let him know my level of disappointment. He was just as disappointed that I wasn't accepting the repairs and that I was "being unreasonable". He needed to get paid and I was causing problems. He insisted that the repairs had been made by his guys. I asked him how he knew that the repairs were made properly when he had not purchased the materials to perform the repairs. I politely told him that he knew the shower surround needed to be removed and completely reinstalled, but he didn't buy them a new surround to install, so he must know the work wasn't done right and he was still trying to bill like the work had been completed correctly. My contractor then decided to inform me as to just how much money he had lost on these last two jobs of mine and that after this he would not be working for me again.

Perhaps if he had been to the properties to perform the bids, he would have either charged more, or at least known what was required of him and his crews. Obviously the job was big enough that a supervisor was required. One of the biggest reasons that the job was taking forever was that he did not allow his crews to carry company cash or credit cards. He provided them with Home Depot gift cards. So anytime they needed materials they had to drive over half an hour to the nearest Home Depot... There was a Lowes one mile away... That's one hour wasted on an eight hour day every time they needed something, because he couldn't get them a gift card to Lowes.

Back to him not wanting to work for me ever again. Finally, something that we could both agree on. I went so far as to tell him he didn't need to work on that house again, and I would be going immediately to check on the progress of the other property. That is when I discovered the very shoddy drywall work. This led to a quick change of locks and a phone call informing him that neither he nor his crews were allowed back on any of my properties.

Now I got to meet the fury of a contractor who wanted payment for work not performed, or at least not performed correctly. He sent me final invoices for both jobs (including the cost of his fines and registration fees), claiming I owed him the full amount of the contracts and demanding immediate payment. We talked and I agreed that I would pay the full amount (*just not all to him*). He liked the conversation up to that point, but when I informed him that I would be deducting the cost of fixing his work from the amount that he would be paid he got upset again. He insisted that I make the payment I had promised. I told him he'd get payment, but that it would be the contract amount, reduced by whatever it cost to have a new contractor fix his work. He went into a complete rage and told me he would see me in court. In a terrible coincidence, we would see each other that night at the investor association meeting. When the meeting ended, he confronted me and demanded payment.

I was calm and showed him and his wife the pictures of his crew's work. He promptly denied that these were pictures of his crew's work and stated that the pictures could have been from anywhere. He became more and more aggressive in his demands for payment and his wife finally made him leave. I was mortified, everyone there was going to think that I was a deadbeat. Several days later I received a call from his wife apologizing and wanting to talk to me about receiving payment. I let her know that there would be no payment as the quotes to fix the poor work were almost as much as their original quote. She was beside herself, she said they needed to get paid and didn't want to go to court but they would take it there if I didn't make full payment.

This is when I played my ace card. I again informed her of the pictures I had of the work and that if this went to court, I would not only win but I would counter sue them. She gave me the same line that her husband had given me that my pictures could have been from any jobsite and that their crews would testify that the pictures were not of their work. Back in the day they may have

126

had a case. Too bad my pictures were taken with my iPhone. Every picture you take with your iPhone is date and location stamped. It didn't matter what they testified to. I had verifiable proof that the pictures were of their work from those houses and after they had invoiced. I think that this may have got her thinking as she ended the call pretty quickly. About an hour later, I received a call from her stating that they had fired the crew and they would not be pursuing payment from me any longer.

I never heard from her or her husband again, and he never attended another investor association meeting again either. I later heard through the grapevine that their business went bankrupt.

Turns out the reason for the problems and the poor work stemmed from some personal problems the contractor was having. Apparently, his son who was the crew leader and supervisor had been severely injured in a motorcycle accident prior to the start of the first project. His son was really the one running the company. When he wasn't there to supervise the crew performance started slowly going down. Once they were aware that no one was going to supervise them ever, they started drinking on the job and their quality and productivity plummeted. Sometimes running a contracting company is just like running an investing business. When it is your money on the line you need to be there.

So much for my idea of contracting things out. What a headache. In the end, it worked out well, as the independent contractor that I had used to come in and fix their mess is now essentially a part time employee of our company. He works for us for one week every month, helping with repairs on existing homes or renovations on new purchases. It seems out of every obstacle or challenge comes some good.

That was the summer from hell, and it was what convinced me that I needed to get out of my job at the mine NOW. I couldn't do that again, my family was suffering from the stress and the missing in action father, and I was letting my business suffer from inattention, which was costing me about as much as I was making at my job. When I went to college I had set a goal for my self of being retired by my age 40. I modified this goal that summer to being self employed by my 35th birthday. Little did I know that with a little help, I would beat that goal.

Chapter 21: Back to Work

Parham and I continued on our path of working maximum hours and trying to do all that we could for the kids at the same time. It was incredibly hard, but we stuck together and made it work, and yes we are still married and best friends. The next year was more of the same, just toned down some on the investing side and ramped up a lot on the work side. At work I was promoted again and put in charge of all of our underground operations. This was a massive undertaking, and pretty much a death sentence for my career.

This promotion required me to do something that our site had not done in a long time, make money. To make a long story short, we failed. As a team our turnover was through the roof, 35% of our salaried employees were leaving every year either voluntarily or not. We were eating people up and spitting them out. When you are losing millions a year with no sign of correction, people either quit or get fired. We had a lot of both of those things going on. Ultimately, we lost about $10 million dollars on a $32 million dollar budget. Things were getting ugly, the company threatened to shut down the facility if we could not figure things out.

Stress levels were high, especially since I could see the light at the end of the tunnel. We were close to getting out of the Rat Race, but we were not quite there. This is when I really started to do the math on what we needed to live off of, as well as what we needed to live off of *and* continue to be able to grow the business. I started researching life and medical insurance costs outside of our employer. I immediately found that I could save 30% on life insurance by buying it independently. This was also more secure as I wouldn't lose it if I lost employment. Check one box off the list. Medical was a big concern, that too was proven to be a fairly easy replacement. Our company employed one of the least healthy workforces in existence, even with my employer paying 80% of the cost we were still shelling out $5,000 per year and had a $6,500 deductible. I hardly even call that insurance. We were responsible for the first $11,500 of costs! Absolutely incredible, it is obvious why health insurance in this country is such a political hot potato. I was paying ~$1,000 per month for insurance. On the open market I was able to find health insurance that was identical to what our company was offering and at a significantly cheaper price. I now pay $550 per month with a $1,500 deductible for the same coverage.

The plan I am with now is one of the few that does not have to accept those with pre-existing conditions and can decide who they accept in and who they don't. People who live healthy lifestyles and take care of themselves are fairly inexpensive to insure. It is when you mandate the coverage of people who don't care about cost, or don't care about living a healthy lifestyle that the cost goes through the roof. At my work we had a lot of both of those along with a very dangerous work environment. This situation combined to make for a very expensive pool of people to insure. Now that I am in a pool of people who chose to live healthy lifestyles, medical expenses have become a lot less expensive, and my path out of the Rat Race got a lot closer.

Our focus on this final year would be to cut our costs to see what it actually took to run the business. Our growth had been so fast, and our expenses were artificially high in many cases due to initial repairs and renovations. We didn't have good numbers to go off of for all of our properties, we needed to figure out what operating costs would be. We had acquired 5 properties that summer and had yet to have good long term cost projections to work from. Additionally, there were costs that we knew that we could reduce by spending more time focusing on efficiency instead of growth. We knew that there were less expensive ways to do many of the things we were doing but with a full-time job and growing the business so fast, it was becoming increasingly difficult to find time for those things. Our time was spent on the growth cycle and not on streamlining things.

Number one on the list of costs to reduce was insurance. This is a product where what you are getting for your money is a commodity, and something that you can't even see for that matter. It doesn't matter what company is servicing your properties, no one will ever know or care who your insurance provider is. As long as your properties are insured, you are good. Now you do need to know the differences in types of insurance, and you need to know what you are buying. There are many forms of coverage and they all have their place in the market. Some plan options include actual cash value, stated value, replacement cost, etc. These are things that you should get familiar with and learn to understand. You can save some money if you move to some of the lesser policies, but you need to recognize that you are saving money because you are taking on more of the risk.

Where you need to look to save money is comparing apples to apples. Don't look at company A's Full Replacement policy and compare it to company B's Stated Value policy. They are two completely different things. Find the type of policy that is best for you, understand the nuances of what is and is not covered and what percent of damages are expected to be paid in a claim, for both partial or full loss. These two things are important and can vary wildly with a full loss paid in full, and a partial loss paid at 50%. Horrifically, I unknowingly had a policy that had those kind of numbers at one point. I would advise that you don't just talk to one insurer, talk to many, and better yet go to a seminar on insurance.

Yes, I know going to an insurance seminar is a pretty boring way to spend a day, but this is your business and you are the CEO (and janitor), you need to be knowledgeable on how much risk you are exposed to. You will learn a lot which will most likely save you thousands down the line. In this business the odds are that at some point you will file a claim. Make sure that you are covered. Also understand that rental property policies vary from homeowner policies in several very important ways.

Homeowner policies cover everything except what they specifically state that they don't cover. Rental policies are the exact opposite, they only cover what they state and nothing else. Understand this, you are exposed to many things that you may not be taking into account. For example, virtually no rental policy will cover water or sewer backups. In the area that I operate in, this was a huge problem for my business. In 2012 there was a very short but intense rain event that caused the storm sewer system to exceed capacity and flood virtually every basement in a multiple square mile area. The damage was amplified by the fact that the city had banned the use of backflow preventers for years, which meant that most homes were completely unprotected from a backup event like this. Many of these properties were rentals, and the damage was not covered by insurance. This led to a significant amount of hobby landlords losing their tenants and walking away from properties because they could not afford to repair the damages on their own. I was able to pick up some properties on the cheap due to their lack of proactivity in educating themselves on insurance.

I have installed backflow preventers on every property I own that has a risk of sewer / storm water backups. Knowing that you are exposed to a risk that is not insured and choosing not to do anything about it is a recipe for disaster.

Another area where we really were able to reduce our operating expenditures was on material costs. Many of you know that Home Depot has a "bid room" for large purchases where you can typically get discounts of 10-15% if you buy all your items for a flip/renovation at once. There are strings attached when you do this, but it is a way to save on cost. Material cost at Home Depot is a big one for us, but we looked at other areas as well.

I set up a meeting with several plumbing companies and was able to negotiate special pricing on all plumbing needs at our properties. I promised to give company A all of our business, and in return they would never charge a service call fee, and they would reduce the hourly rate that they charged by 13%. We also pay cost for all materials used, which means there are no mark ups! That not only has put more money in my pocket, but I get a better service as they see me as a premier customer.

At the same time, we set up commercial accounts with several supply houses. We are now able to by all flooring products directly from the largest distributor in the state. This has resulted in major savings. There are no middlemen markups, and they even gave us a list of independent installers. Again, major savings on projects. These were just some of the ways that we were able to reduce our operating costs and become more efficient.

As this critical year in our business development cycle progressed, we were able to realize cost savings of over $10,000 per year as a result of these various business agreements. To put it another way, we reduced our costs by roughly 10%. Now that we were able to step back and focus on costs versus growth, we were in a better position to grow our business. We were also in a better position to compete in the marketplace as our costs have moved to below that of our competitors. Simply put, we are the low-cost producer and we can beat our competitors due to their higher cost structure. Most importantly, we were more profitable and all $10,000 of those savings went right to our bottom line, meaning that was $10,000 less income that we would need when our W-2 income went away.

Our W-2 income did end up going away in 2016, and when it did, we were prepared. Ultimately, it went away 7 months and 8 days earlier than our plan, but that was ok. We had 21 rental units bringing in just over $200,000 per year. Several amazing things happened once that W-2 income disappeared. Almost every bank on the planet decided that they no longer wanted to loan us money, even the bank that we had been using for years and had a great relationship with. Also, I learned a very valuable lesson: when you don't have any options, you create opportunities. We got creative and started doing something that we should have done years earlier: using owner financing. We were established enough that other investors were able to recognize that we knew what we were doing and were willing to owner finance us their properties as long as we would take care of their headaches.

These owners had problems that they needed resolved. They didn't need money; they needed solutions to the complex problems that they were facing. We presented ourselves to them as an answer to their problems. Within six months we took over three commercial multi-family properties, all owner financed. The owner financing part was the simplest part of the entire transaction. The owner of two of the properties that we purchased flew in on a $3.5 million dollar private jet to sign the documents to sell his apartments to us. He didn't need the money, he could have cared less about the money. He cared about his business and his family, and these were two areas that these buildings were causing big problems in. Selling them solved his problems. This gentleman had divided his business into parts and had given his children control over the different parts. One child had grown his part of the business into a multi-million dollar company that was very successful, another had not grown her part of the business at all and was in fact stealing from the business. To make matters worse, the fighting between the children was at the point of being destructive to his family.

His solution was to sell off the parts of the business that were nonperforming. This allowed him to let go of the parts of the business that harbored his kids that weren't doing well. This solution allowed the one remaining profitable division to be able to grow without distraction. How did this benefit him? Well for starters, he didn't have to have the conversation with his kids to let them know that he no longer wanted them working for the family business. He simply had to tell them that he was retiring and cashing out. The division that was ran successfully would stay running as that child had made arrangements to buy it. In fact, to be fair he had given all of his kids the opportunity to purchase the divisions that they ran. Turns out the kids that were not doing well running their divisions were not interested in purchasing them. His child that was excelling was able to obtain owner financing...

I was one of the lucky benefactors of this, all I had to do was buy a half empty six unit building that hadn't been updated in 40 years, and a vacant quad that was in a rough part of town. The owner recognized that these properties were difficult sell and was willing to price them at a point that would be worth the headache. Having been in the business, he knew how much of a headache they would be to get up and running, so we really didn't need to haggle over pricing at all. Today those two buildings are the single most profitable properties that we own. He priced them based on their performance and potential. His idea of potential was a little skewed as he had owned them for 40+ years and was not up to speed on how much rents had changed. He was using rent numbers that were probably five years old, or $50-$100 per unit less than market.

The third commercial property that we bought involved bringing my brother in 50/50 on the deal. The "owner" in that scenario was about 65 years old who did not want to inherit the property. Her mother, the actual owner, was in poor health and had not been maintaining the property for some time. It was infested with roaches, and in terrible condition but its location was a prime. Best of all the bones were great, it just needed major upgrading, virtually all new tenants and a good exterminator. The daughter wanted to make certain that the property was sold before her mother died and she inherited it.

Due to the poor condition of the property and the fact that she had been keeping the books in a manner that showed it losing money every year, it was no longer loanable. She had to seller finance it. This is why you should run your business as a business and not as a hobby. Her greed in cheating Uncle Sam out of tax dollars cost her children significant inheritance. When you get into a situation where the banks won't loan on your properties, you are not helping yourself. She had to owner finance.

Now she just needed to find someone that she could trust, someone that could operate the property effectively and deal with the problems they were getting. She really wanted to make sure that we could deal with the problems as she didn't want them back. We presented her an offer that met her needs and put us in a position to have good cashflow. We agreed that she would hold the note for just over two years so that we could get two years of tax returns showing a profit, from there we would refinance it. This worked out perfectly in the end. Our purchase price and payment to her was low enough that over those two years all repairs and upgrades were performed from the cash flow that the

136

property was generating. At the end of the two years, we applied to refinance the property and it appraised for $300,000 more than we purchased it for! Not a bad transaction. This property is, was and continues to be a management headache, but it is also generating considerable cash flow allowing us to continue to grow our business.

Think about how much money was lost by failing to put money back into a business. We performed approximately $40,000 in repairs in those two years and received $300,000 in equity gains. If her mother had made that $40,000 investment in her business instead of taking the money out of the business, her daughter would have had significantly more inheritance. Not only that perhaps her daughter would have kept the building as the tenant management is always made simpler with a building in good repair.

By the end of 2016, and without any W-2 income, we had gone from 21 rental units to 45 rental units. This should tell you everything that you need to know about the need to focus entirely on your business. I had been focusing on someone else's business to the detriment of my own. This more than proved to me how much more we could grow the business if we focused on it exclusively. In seven months, we more than doubled the size of our business, and we did this all without any W-2 income or commercial loans. Can you imagine how fast we would have built the business had we been focusing on it full-time for the three and a half years leading up to this? Talk about a hard pill to swallow. How much family time and money had I missed out on working for a company that I couldn't stand for 3 years, when I should have been working for myself? Lesson learned; I will never hold a W-2 job again.

Now that we were out of the Rat Race, things really started to improve. We were able to actually take time to go on vacation, our first real trip in years. We went camping in Acadia National Park in Maine. It was awesome, as a family we had a great time and have memories that will last forever. I don't know what was more impressive my 4 year old daughter Caroline hiking up Cadillac Mountain all by herself without ever complaining or my two year old sleeping through the entire hike while being carried on our backs. I will never forget that hike up Cadillac Mountain with the kids or camping with a crib in the tent. Life was starting to get much better. We finally had some semblance of financial independence, and personal freedom.

Chapter 22: Self-Employed Life:

Life changes quite a bit when you become self-employed. The first major change for me was no longer waking up at 6:00 am to go to work. It takes a while to get comfortable with the fact that there is nothing wrong with sleeping in a bit. In fact, with kids it becomes almost a necessity. I committed to spending more time with our kids now that I had more time. I also still needed to work, but I could work on my schedule and not someone else's. I decided that I would put the kids on the bus every morning. I know the kids appreciate this, and I definitely know that my wife appreciates help with getting everyone ready in the morning. It works out for me pretty well too, as most of my job duties can't start at 7:00 am anyways. I mean you can't go working on tenants' houses, or look at properties, or really do any construction work at that hour. So now I sleep in later and help out in the mornings.

I do stay up later which works out nicely as my wife and I tend to do our office work and keep the books after we put the kids to bed. So, my day now looks something like this: get up at 7:30, get kids on the bus at 8:30, go to work, be home by 3:30 to get the kids off of the bus and family time until 8:30. Then I start back on office work from 8:30pm to 10:30pm. I am working 8 hours a day, but they are the 8 hours that I choose. If one of the kids has a field trip, or a function at school that I need to attend I simply don't schedule that time. I can make it up on the weekend, or maybe one day I don't get the kids off the bus and I work a little later. Either way, my life is now centered around my family's schedule and not my employer's schedule.

I never really understood the 40 hour work week schedule for salaried employees. There were parts of the year when the workload was well under 40 hours per week, but we still had to be at the site for 40 hours. There were significant parts of the year where the work load was 60 hours per week. We worked 60 hours those weeks. I would have really appreciated the opportunity to relax and rejuvenate during the slow times so I could be better during the hard times. Besides we were only being paid for 40 hours a week, those 60 hour weeks could have been offset and were not.

Another huge plus that has come from exiting the Rat Race is that I have become an active member of the community. I volunteer with the local soccer club (commissioner for the U7/U8 age group and coach), I frequently attend our city council meetings and my wife is president of the PTA. None of this community involvement would have been possible if I had continued in management at a large corporation. I remember my boss once saying about a promotion that the salary was increasing, and the hourly wage was decreasing. That's the way management works; the more they pay you, the less time you have for your family and your community. It is a poor trade off and you should not make it if you can help it. By getting a real estate education through the Great Lakes REIA, I was able to gain the skills to get out of that poor trade that I had made.

Another major change that you have to get used to when you are self-employed is that no one can comprehend that you still work. It really gets to me at times, but after a couple of years most of my friends seem to finally understand that both my wife and I do actually have jobs and that we do work. They don't really understand what it is that we do, but they at least understand that we don't just sit at home all day eating bonbons.

The biggest problem is the people that are more acquaintances and neighbors, as they really have no clue about our lifestyle and work. I can't tell you how many times my wife has been asked to watch someone's kids during the day. Several times people have offered to pay her, assuming that she would like the extra spending money. We pay a sitter one day per week to watch Carson our little one who is not in school yet so that Parham can have a full day to work in the office. People just can't imagine that she is actually busy during the day. Running a business is a full-time job, for both my wife and I. People miss that part. My wife is frequently asked to go out for coffee in the mornings with the moms from the preschool. This is her only time during the day without kids! It is her time to get the work done that she can't do when the kids are around. None of these stay at home moms understand that she isn't a stay at home mom, she is a self-employed mom. Her time is immensely valuable as there is very little of it. Be prepared for the confusion that being self employed causes those who can't see anything beyond a nine to five.

I get the same sort of requests, but mine are mostly from people wanting to buy me lunch and spend time asking questions about real estate. Sure, I like a free lunch and I like helping others, but these requestors don't seem to understand that my time is valuable to me. Most seem to think that since I own a lot of rental properties and don't have a W-2 job, that I am retired and have tons of free time. That couldn't be further from the truth. I am a busy person and meeting someone half an hour away for a one-hour lunch completely kills my productivity for that day. To me, a lunch meeting means I can't get started on any major work because I have to be cleaned up and gone by 11:30am. It also means I can't get any major work done in the afternoon because I won't be able to get to the job site until 1:30 and then I have to turn around and be home to get the kids off of the bus at 3:30pm. These lunch meetings kill my days. I love helping others and sharing my stories. However, it kills me when people assume that I have tons of time.

Other requests that I get are to simply hand people all of my contacts, again I don't mind helping people out, and I am more than happy to share a contact or two, but there becomes a point where I feel that I'm just being used. These people are not truly trying to build a business, they are on the "get rich quick" plan that inevitably fails, because they don't want to do the hard work for themselves. I am now very hesitant to give out contacts, as this frequently results in the requestor calling me to complain about the contractor's work. My contractors are good, but they need management and contracts. I can give out the contact, but I can't do the management or write the contract for you.

A further change that comes with being self-employed is the necessity of focusing on time management as it is easy to get sidetracked and end up wasting a day. We have a home office, which we consider to be both a blessing and a curse. The blessing is that we can work on business items after the kids go to bed or for a few minutes here and there when the kids are occupied. We can even get stuff done quickly on the weekends without having to run out. The curse is that it is easy to get distracted when working at home, and if the kids have off from school you end up getting nothing done in the office.

Hopefully, with time, we can make a more formal office in our home. We didn't buy a home with a space for a home office, so currently our dining room serves this makeshift purpose. This is cumbersome and we will have to address it sooner rather than later. The other part of the curse of a home office is our four year old. He does not quite understand that the copier is not a toy, or that the papers on the desk are not for coloring on. There have been more than a few documents that have gone out with coloring on them. Luckily, most people seem to understand.

Yet another true blessing of being self-employed is the freedom around scheduling vacations. The days of waiting for long weekends or for an employer's approval are a thing of the past. We can take advantage of heavy discounts on travel costs that are offered to those traveling at off peak times. We recently saved about 25% on plane tickets by leaving on a Saturday and coming home on a Tuesday. My sister and her husband are self-employed as well, which has allowed us to meet up on vacations and take advantage of these savings. Better yet, my dad is retired so really the whole family can meet up and take advantage of this, only my brother is still tethered to a day job, and that tether will break here pretty soon, as he too has had quite a bit of success in real estate.

Chapter 23: Trials and Tribulations

Our business tripled in size within 28 months and quintupled in size within 36 months of becoming self-employed. With that kind of growth, we have seen quite a bit more and had some unbelievable experiences. Unexpected, unimaginable and challenging experiences just come with the territory of being an investor. Here are a few of our more outrageous tenant episodes.

Shortly after investing full-time, we placed a fairly mature and newly engaged couple into one of our homes. The lady in the relationship, Vicky, had worked for the county government for 28 years. Vicky didn't make a fortune, but she clearly made enough to afford the rent. The gentleman in the relationship, Chuck, was a forklift driver currently off of work due to a recent surgery. Things started out well enough, then there was a late payment, followed by another late payment. Payments continued to be late for some time and we continued to work with Vicky and Chuck as they were clearly struggling. Vicky was always open and honest with us and communicated well. Our frustration with the late rent was mounting, but the light at the end of the tunnel for them (and us) was the fact that Chuck was going to be heading back to work soon. Which he did, well kind of.

Chuck went back to work for a week and then went off again for another surgery. Rents continued to be late but they always got paid, just a bit of a pain but not the end of the world. This story repeated itself as Chuck ended up having two knee replacements, a hip replacement and a major surgery on his rotator cuff. This guy was determined not to work and seemed perfectly fine letting his sugar mama pay all the bills. Vicky, the sugar mama, became more and more depressed as Chuck contributed less and less to their finances, and presumably did less and less at home.

Finally, Vicky ran away. I received an urgent call from Chuck asking me to come change the locks. He wanted the locks changed so that she couldn't take any of his stuff if she came back while he wasn't home. The last thing I needed was to be caught up in their mess. I told him he was on his own, she was on the lease and I wasn't changing the locks. Well, Vicky did eventually come home. Apparently, she ran out of money and came back three days later. At this point, we served them with a three-day notice to move out or pay rent.

I was now officially done with their mess. Our three-day notice led Vicky to attempt to kill herself by overdosing on pills. Chuck proceeded to let me know that my selfish demand for money had sent her over the edge. Getting blamed for your tenant's money problems happens a lot in this business, so if you want to be a landlord you should develop thick skin. To me it is water off a duck's back, I can listen to it and disagree and move on. I know that I didn't do anything wrong, and that I was more patient with them than most landlords would ever have been. I was allowing them to pay late on a regular basis, as I knew their situation was rough, and I didn't want to make life any harder on them. Now I was paying the price of trying to be a good person. If I had evicted them at the get-go, when payments were late, I would have never had to listen to the tirades of one belligerent Chuck. Setting the precedent of accepting late rent can be very bad as it was in this case. I did it because Vicky was a good person, and I believed their situation would improve. When it was obvious that it wouldn't we stopped. Chuck was right I did have some responsibly in this but it had nothing to do with us being greedy, in fact it was the exact opposite. If I had been greedy and less tolerant, I never would have had to deal with that mess, some other

145

poor dumb landlord would have. But I didn't and the Chuck and Vicky story continues.

Vicky survived the suicide attempt, but was placed into an institution for two weeks for a mental health evaluation. The institution they placed her in is located right next to a hospital and along U.S. Route 20. As soon as she was let out of the institution, she immediately bolted as fast as she could across the parking lot, down the driveway and right into the four-lane highway. She ran out in front of the first car coming down the road and got flattened! Don't worry readers Vicky survived being hit by the car. She had some serious road rash, a few broken ribs, and two working legs. She used these two working legs to run from the scene of the accident and hide out in the parking lot of an adjacent apartment building while the police and EMT's searched for her.

Something tells me they should not have cleared her for release from that institution. There are a lot problems with mental health in this country and the institutions that we place people into are definitely an area to improve upon.

Vicky survived her second suicide attempt, but was worse for wear. They took her to the hospital next door this time to treat the road rash that she had picked up and the broken ribs. Her next journey was from the hospital back to the institution. She spent another two weeks there. By this point Chuck had paid their rent in full to avoid eviction. I was almost hoping that the eviction would just go forward so that we could be done, and I would no longer be forced to be a part of their drama. I am a busy person and lord knows I don't want to be spending my time dealing with these types of issues, and the risks associated with people who have unstable minds.

Vicky was released from the institution again after another two-week stay. Something tells me that must be the limit that you can be kept against your will. Once she got out, Chuck took two weeks off of work to help supervise her and make sure that she was not going to hurt herself again. This worked fairly well, but it turns out he was the reason for all of the problems. According to the neighbors, he was emotionally abusive to her. They told me story after story about how he would belittle her and yell at her for little to no reason. I wish the neighbor had let me in on their relationship problems earlier rather than later. After two weeks of supervising her, Chuck had to go back to work. Vicky enjoyed a last day of freedom from him, and then went into the bathroom and poured a glass of gasoline on herself. Right before he was to get off work, she lit herself on fire in the bathroom.

I can only imagine how intense the pain must have been. She ran from the bathroom, through the house in a big circle and then outside where the neighbor saw her and tackled her to the ground, smothering her and the fire.

I can't imagine ever being put in that situation. The neighbor acted quickly and appropriately in an attempt to save her. He and most of the people who lived on that street were pretty traumatized by witnessing this event. He yelled for help and another neighbor called 911. As he was trying to help her, she was screaming in pain and yelling that she was still burning. As the neighbor went to get more help and blankets, she got up and ran towards Lake Erie where she fell and rolled down the 15 foot embankment and into the lake. Our rental house is/was only about 150 feet from the shore. By the time emergency services got there, she had been pulled out of the lake by the neighbor. She was still alive but in very poor condition with most of her skin melted off of her. She was airlifted straight to the burn unit of a hospital, where she spent her final 4 weeks of life. This was all in all a terrible experience for everyone involved. I wish that I had not been a part of it in anyway. You will have experiences in this business that you never asked for or wanted.

Experiences like this are rare but stay in the industry long enough and they will happen. The scenarios you experience may not be as bad as this one was, but you will eventually experience everything imaginable and then some.

Another one of those "once in a lifetime" experiences that we have been through was our battle with Lew. The quad that we bought in a "not so great" part of town had a problem, and it has started a mini war with Mr. Lew, dictator of ordinance enforcement. The second tenant that we put in our vacant quad seemed decent. She had poor credit, but otherwise she seemed ok. Her boyfriend who moved in with her, however, was a piece of work. Once he moved in, he convinced her that she didn't need to pay rent. He had somehow gotten it in his mind that since the apartment was not perfect, he would not need to pay rent.

The event that had made the apartment "not perfect" was a three day period where the building had a sewer leak. We addressed the problem as quickly and professionally as possible. However, he was demanding a free month of rent for the inconvenience. I tried and tried to explain to him he would not be receiving a free month of rent, and his response was that I was rich and could afford it. I am not rich, I work hard for my money and didn't intend to give it away, especially to this guy. Furthermore, I am not going to set the precedent that every time something goes wrong that my tenants get free rent. Our last conversation went quickly, I told him he could be out by the end of the week and we wouldn't go after them for the rent or we could proceed with an eviction. He chose to go the eviction route.

Before we could evict him, he managed to beat the stuffing out of someone coming to collect money from him that he owed them. That, of course, led to an arrest warrant. So, after the court order to evict them both, but prior to the sheriff showing up to actually throw them out, he was set to be arrested. When the police came to arrest him, he decided that he didn't want to go to jail. His girlfriend decided that she did want to go to jail, so he and his girlfriend locked themselves into the house, and proceeded to get into a standoff with the police. The police were amazingly considerate and simply called me to see if I would bring them a key to let them into the apartment. They really didn't want to break in the door, and I didn't want them to either, so I obliged and brought them a key. I also informed them that there was a nice crisp one hundred dollar bill to whoever accidentally bumped his head a few times in getting him out of the house and into a patrol car. But alas they didn't want to do the paperwork associated with that. Instead, they opened the door and let the police dog into the unit. Our tenant's boyfriend came out pretty quickly after that.

Now I just needed to apologize to all of my other tenants in the building that had to spend the better part of an evening evacuated from their units. Having a police standoff at one of your rental properties is probably a sign that you have messed up somewhere along the way. Lesson learned. Now that the tenants were in jail, I received the privilege of having to put all of their belongings onto the tree lawn as per the eviction's stipulation. That jerk didn't even bother to move his crap out before getting his 16 year invite to the state pen.

The bailiff showed up at 8:30 in the morning to return possession of the apartment to us. We immediately started putting all of their belongings out onto the tree lawn. At 9:30 the city ordinance inspector showed up and wrote us a $250 fine for placing litter on the tree lawn. Another $500 fine associated with the city's removal of the "litter" on the tree lawn was issued the next morning. That's right, you can always count on the

149

government ~~to do the right thing~~ to try and squeeze a dollar out of you.

I can't believe that the city inspector was out following the bailiff around writing citations all morning. Talk about unethical. Yes, they actually had a copy of the bailiff's eviction schedule for the day (in this area all evictions are performed on the same day in the city). The court order required us to leave the tenants' belongings on the tree lawn for 24 hours, yet here was the city, one hour later, writing us a fine for obeying a court order. Unbelievable. Furthermore, the city was out cleaning up the mess less than 24 hours after it was made, while we were still under court order to keep it there. It amazes me how the city can clean up a mess within 24 hours when they think they will get paid $500 to do 45 minutes of work. When they make a mess and have to clean it up on their dime, it takes months. They recently cut down two trees on this very same section of tree lawn, it took over 5 months for the city to remove the debris, and that only happened after multiple complaints to the city.

Back to my $750 bill from the city. Readers, don't worry, I wasn't going to stand for these BS fines. If nothing else, I stand up for my rights and will not let Uncle Sam pick my pockets any more than legally required. I proceeded to let the city inspector know what I thought of the fines and that I believed they should be dropped as they would never stand up in court. Following the bailiff around is just reprehensible in my opinion. The inspector basically told me where to stick it and that I would be paying the fine because I violated city ordinances by putting the tenants' belongings on the tree lawn. She stated quite clearly that the fact that the court ordered the placing of the belongings on the tree lawn was irrelevant to the citation.

Ordinances were ordinances, and I needed to pay my fine just like all the others. Well that did not go over very well with me. I proceeded to call her boss, the Assistant City Manager Mr. Lew, who basically told me the same thing. He informed me that if I would have done a better job of finding tenants, then I would not have had this problem. Again, while I appreciated the advice, it still didn't sit well with me. After some investigating, I discovered that the city is required to give me 24 hours' notice to correct violations before they can issue fines. The notice of ordinance violation that the city sent had clearly arrived after the problems were cited and cleaned up. Their date stamps even indicated that they were not sent out 24 hours before they cleaned up the mess. With this in my back pocket, I called Lew back and asked him to reconsider the fines.

Mr. Lew ultimately declined to waive the fines and I informed him that I would be contesting the fines in court. I also informed him that I would be appearing before the very same judge who issued the order to put the items on the tree lawn. I doubt that a judge would find me guilty of a crime when the crime involved following his order to a tee. In the end, the city relented and waived the fines, and I agreed to pay only the dump fees at the land fill as I would have had to pay those had I been allowed to haul the items away myself. This event has led to a very long and protracted battle with Lew and his department, one in which I finally appear to be winning I would like to add.

Lew, who doesn't even live in the city, drives passed my property on his way to and from work every day. This has led to him personally issuing violations to my business. We had an ice storm in January one year, and a section of gutter came down. We live in northeast Ohio, these things happen. Two days later, however, I received a letter in the mail from my friends in the ordinance department letting me know that I had a gutter down and that it needed to be fixed. The letter itself isn't what bothered me, what really bothered and truly astounded me was the fact that somehow my building was the only one on the street that managed to get such a nice letter in the mail. The building to the south of mine had been abandoned for over 5 years, yet it didn't receive any citations for its gutter violations. I guess it isn't worth their time to give citations to the owners of abandoned buildings. Seems to me those are the kinds of buildings the city should be addressing. The building to the north of mine didn't even have gutters, yet the owner occupants of that building did not receive any gutter violations either. Only my building received citations, imagine that. We fixed the gutter.

A couple weeks later, we received another letter in the mail with regards to a tenant parking on the lawn during the snow ban. A snow ban is when the city bans parking along the street so that they can plow the roads. My building is a four-unit building with only four parking spots (nose to tail). I am not the one who approved the zoning for a four-unit building with only four parking spots. One of my tenants, who works night shift, gets home at 4:00am, and if he parks in the driveway, he gets woken up at 7:00am to move his car so the others can get out. Normally he parks on the street, but when they banned parking on the street he parked in the yard. My thought was that this would be a police issue as they are the only ones that can issue parking tickets in the city. Of course, the police department has real problems to worry about and this is not one of them. They can hardly justify spending time writing $10 parking tickets when there is real crime to deal with.

Now Lew, on the other hand, doesn't have any real work to do so he had plenty of time to issue me a $300 fine as parking in the yard is also a zoning violation, which his department covers. After several conversations with my city councilwoman and the city manager, it was agreed that the city would remove the trees from the tree lawn, and I would install a second driveway. The

152

house is on a corner and the primary driveway is on the street that the house does not face. Every house on the street that the house faces has a driveway on that street but mine. Seemed to my Councilwoman, the City Manager, and I to be a pretty simple fix to a pretty simple problem.

Now enter Mr. Lew… The city somewhat upheld their portion of the agreement. They cut down the trees and ground the stumps, but they left all of the cuttings and debris on the tree lawn for me to haul away. When I applied for a permit to add the agreed upon driveway, it was denied. Mr. Lew informed me that since my multi-family building was zoned as a single-family building, I could not add parking. The city does not allow properties that do not conform to zoning codes to be improved upon, and adding a driveway would improve the property.

This was very frustrating as the building was a multi-family property before the city had zoning codes. Additionally, the City Manager had signed off on adding a driveway. These facts did not seem to hold any influence on Mr. Lew or the Zoning Department.

Yet again, I found myself amazed at our asinine ordinances. How could it be that I wasn't allowed to add parking? My councilwoman and the City Manager were in favor of parking being added to the property. I was going to have to file an appeal to the Board of Zoning Appeals to get a hearing on the matter. This involved paying a $200 fee and waiting a couple of months for the next board meeting.

In the meantime, my apartment building just down the road was continuing to have problems with the neighbors using our dumpster. The neighbors didn't have trash service and for years had been using our dumpster. Normally this wouldn't be a problem, but the neighbor's son got a construction job and was constantly dumping construction debris into the dumpster and overflowing it. After about $500 worth of overflow charges by my friends at Waste Management, we finally had to notify the neighbors that they could no longer use our dumpster. Of course, they completely failed to stop using our dumpster. One day, after watching them put a set of tires into it, I finally went to Mr. Lew's office to complain. I explained that the neighbors didn't have trash service, and that this was a city ordinance violation for which I needed Mr. Lew's office to take corrective action. Mr. Lew's office, of course, did nothing as the neighbors were owner occupants and the city has a policy about citing owner occupants. The policy is that they don't do it. Finally, the last straw came one night when I was on my way to a city council meeting and one of my tenants called me to tell me that the neighbor had just dumped an entire pickup truck load of trash on the ground next to the dumpster. (The dumpster was full) He even had pictures of them doing it. What a crappy neighbor, simply unloaded a truckload of trash onto our parking lot...

I called the police and asked them if they would have a talk with the neighbors, hoping maybe this would finally get the point across. I did not press charges or anything of the sort, I just wanted the neighbors to stop using our dumpster. The following morning I received another call from my tenant, the city ordinance officer was at the property walking around taking pictures. (It is against policy for ordinance officers to step foot on peoples property without their permission, but who's counting) Mr. Lew proceeded to issue me a citation for having litter on my property. What a piece of work, and people wonder why the city is having trouble attracting investors. I even received another citation for a tenant having expired tags on their car.

How is it my problem that a tenant has expired tags? Isn't that a police issue if they are driving around on expired tags? Apparently, that too is a zoning violation that can be issued to the property owner. This led to a call to my Councilwoman and the City Manager who informed me that she would be having a talk with Mr. Lew. I told her he needed more than a talk, as far as I was concerned this was harassment. My property was targeted due to a grudge that Mr. Lew was carrying. I was told that this wasn't the case, that the ordinance officer simply was responding to the police complaint and while they were there, they wrote the citations that they saw.

Color me crazy if I didn't believe this for one second. My neighbor, the one who was dumping the trash onto my property, had not received any citations. Not a single one. Mr. Lew and company apparently didn't see that he had a broken-down car parked in the front yard, less than 30 feet from the area where they had written me up for litter. They also apparently didn't see the missing gutters on his house, or anything else they could've easily chosen to cite. I asked the city manager to see the records from my complaint about them not having trash service and that I wanted to know what the city had done to resolve this complaint. I never heard back from the City Manager on this, but I thought that I got my point across.

Back to the zoning appeal, after months of waiting I finally had my hearing. Mr. Lew was there, and it did not look as though my request for additional parking would be granted. The City lawyer testified that the City's position was that the building needed to be converted from an apartment building to a single family home due to not meeting zoning code. Really? I thought the building was there before his code. After about 20 mins of being grilled, I finally told the board, "look, the city has already removed the trees and ground out the stumps for this project. We can go forward or not." The head of the appeals board stopped me and asked directly if he had heard me right, that the city was on board and had removed their trees so that the project could go forward. I responded, "yes."

At that point, Mr. Lew interjected that that was not quite accurate and that while the city had removed the trees, it had nothing to do with my putting in a driveway. I was flabbergasted, I didn't even know what to say, this was an out-right lie under sworn testimony. I was able to prove he had lied too. I had copies of emails from Mr. Lew to the City Manager explicitly stating that the trees were being removed for the additional driveway. The next week I had a nice meeting with the City Manager again. I showed up with his testimony and a copy of his emails. I don't know what was said after that meeting with the City Manager, but Mr. Lew has been nothing but nice to me since. He even went so far as to let me know of a property that I may want to purchase.

I sincerely hope the point may have finally gotten across that there are good landlords operating in the city, and that his department needs to be helping them and not harassing them. There are plenty of slumlords that they should be addressing. Remember, all of this fighting with the city over a two year period started because a tenant moved in her criminal boyfriend who convinced her not to pay rent. Truth be told, I should have done a much better job of setting ground rules and expectations with the tenant before handing her the keys, as she ultimately caused me many headaches over a period of two years. Worst yet, she was only a tenant for four months! These are the types of things you will deal with as a landlord, if you are not prepared to deal with them, don't get into the business.

One thing you should know is that evictions will follow your tenants. About 18 months after the fact, my tenant that put me through two years of hell with the city called me up trying to find out why there was a $5,000 judgement against her. She had applied to buy a car, and couldn't buy it due to the judgement against her that came with the eviction. I was hoping that this meant that she wanted to make payment, but no she just wanted me to forgive the debt as it was "all her former boyfriend's fault, and he was in jail." Believe me, I didn't feel one bit sorry that she couldn't get her car.

One final war story that I have is of a disabled tenant of mine. We have one property that houses disabled members of the community. I thought that it was going to really be great getting into that niche of land lording. After all who does not want to be able to help disabled children. We would be providing a much-needed service to the community and were really able to make a positive impact in the life of these disabled kids. Our property is adjacent to a facility designed to help children with special needs. What a perfect opportunity. How could this go wrong.

Well ignorance is bliss only while you are ignorant. After getting into this part of the business we quickly became aware of the level of care that these people were receiving and of the difficulties that they face on a daily basis. I have never been so ashamed and appalled. I did not get into the business to see children be abused and neglected but that is what basically goes on in these homes. And it is now going on in one of our homes. I want nothing more to do with it, but I know that if I move these people out the abuse will just happen elsewhere. The support system for fully disabled people in our society is terrible. The care givers get paid around $12 per hour to "provide care". For the most part they just sit in the house and watch TV while the client sleeps. Most of these disabled kids will sleep for excessive amounts of time, or just stare at walls/lava lamps for hours on end. Not a great quality of life. But they do have their moments of happiness. And they can definitely teach us a lot about gratitude. I am very grateful of what I have and of the gifts that I have been given. I have three healthy and amazing kids that I am so thankful for. When one of our kids is struggling I just think how much harder it could be.

Back to the dismal levels of care that these people receive. Often these people do not have functional coping systems for when they get agitated or frustrated. When this occurs, is when the care givers earn their pay. They must protect the children from themselves. Often the disabled children will injure themselves when they are agitated. The care givers are there to step in and prevent this. Only problem is if they are downstairs watching TV when the person gets agitated upstairs then they are only able to respond to the injury as they can not react fast enough to prevent the person from injuring themselves. I have had to repair a lot of damage due to negligent care, and have had to hear the stories of how people were injured or attacked while in my property. All while we the taxpayers are shelling out massive amounts of money to provide quality care for these kids who deserve nothing but the best.

Recently I had a report of a backed-up drain at this property. When I got there to deal with the problem I found that the drain was clogged with paper towels. Paper towels with condoms wrapped up in them… This is a property that is used to house disabled children… (The staff of the house is supposed to be all female, as all the kids in the house are non-verbal teenage girls) I was sick to my stomach at what I found and had to immediately report it to the Board of Developmental Disabilities. Eventually the police had to investigate as there was the potential rape of a child involved. Their investigation lasted less than an hour. The child's parent did not want her child to have to go through a rape test as it would be traumatic to her. The child cannot speak so there is no victim to complain. The State really did not have a ton of concern as neither the child nor her parent were filing a criminal complaint. There is essentially no public advocate for these kids. In the end I suspect it was the staff inviting friends over for sex while they were supposed to be watching the children, but still that is a serious issue. Maybe that is why the children keep ending up injured because the staff isn't doing their job. Instead of watching the kids they are inviting there boyfriends over to have sex on our taxpayer's time. It really tears me up to think about these things going on in a property that I own. On too many occasions I have had to be the advocate for these children. I can only imagine what goes on when I am not there. I have had to report abuse at this house on too many occasions. Can you imagine as this is just one of these houses; it is a single data point in a system of hundreds of these houses. Anyone who has children should be horrified and concerned about the care system for severely disabled individuals. Please do not go into this sector of the business if you have trouble compartmentalizing things or are just an overly empathetic human.

While I may only have a few of these kind of war stories, it is still more than I want to have. Doing the extra work on the front end can really help you manage to avoid too many of these situations. There are other investors in my group that have stories that make mine look like kid games. Be prepared to deal with events like this if you want to be in the rental business.

Chapter 24: Cost of Growth

As we reached the 60 rental unit level, we are still a small and growing business but we are a business, and we need to operate like one. As we have grown, expenses crop up that were not there when we started the business. Things such as taxes become significantly more important and time consuming. When we first started, we could use simple online software to do our taxes. It worked great for us and didn't cost very much. As more properties were purchased and the LLC was formed, we found ourselves in a new position. I couldn't get the taxes done to the level that I needed with off the shelf software.

We needed to hire an actual accountant. These people cost real money, and they are usually worth the price you pay. We interviewed multiple accountants and ended up changing accountants twice before we found someone that not only did we trust, but we knew understood our business. This firm clearly understood accounting like all of the others, but they really seemed to understand where we had come from and could follow our vision for the future. Jeff, one of the principle accountants at the firm, sat down with us and pointed out challenges that would come with some of our growth. He and his employees were also able to provide practical solutions to those challenges. Jeff and his firm not only shared our vision, but most importantly they saw us as long term customers. They understood that the more successful they could help us become, the more business we would be able to give them. It has truly been a mutually beneficial relationship. Having trusted advisors is incredibly important. I now call my accountant before making major business decisions just to get a feel for how my taxes and costs will be affected.

Some transactions don't make any difference as far as taxes to Uncle Sam go, but they do make a big difference for the accountant that is preparing the tax returns. I recently had one of these transactions, and I was very glad I called and got advice before writing an offer on a property. I was able to structure the transaction in a manner that did not affect my tax position at all, but did make it much easier on my tax preparer. This equals money saved, the cleaner I can make things for the accountants the less I have to pay them. It also means that when we get big enough to hire full-time help, it will be easier to get the new hire up to speed as the business will be set up the right way.

Accounting is just one small part of the office work that actually becomes work as your business grows. Bookkeeping and invoicing will quickly become a bear unless you can get a system in place that works for you early on. Many companies offer software to assist with the bookkeeping end of things. Again, when you are just starting out it is really hard to justify the cost of this software, especially if you only have a handful of properties. As you grow though, bookkeeping will become very intensive and you should have a system in place that accounts for all money in and all money out. Your system should also account for money *not* in, for example past due rents, late fees, etc.

Our system is really great, and it has taken years to get to the point it is at. It took me years of back and forth with my wife, but we finally agreed on a system that works for both of us. Our system basically works like this: I don't touch anything, and I am given access to nothing. We both agree that this is the system we will use going forward. It could use some automation, but all in all it works well. You should not be the president, CEO, accountant, treasurer, etc. You will need a backstop in place at some point if for nothing else than to keep you in check. Parham does a great job of keeping me in check and forecasting expenses and revenues which is much needed as I tend to buy, buy, buy. And she points out major expenses coming up, such as the upcoming tax payment of $20,000, etc.

Back to the bookkeeping system. We worked hand in hand developing what we have. I built a spreadsheet when we very first started out, and it worked for me. As our number of properties grew, it got a little cumbersome. I had made some improvements here and there, and taught Parham how to use it as well, she hated it. Once we started running our business as a business, it no longer worked at all. When we formally started our business, Parham took over the bookkeeping and immediately started making changes to our spreadsheet. Each year as our business has grown, and our needs have expanded, Parham has improved the spreadsheet to capture and provide more and more information. Currently, we still use this spreadsheet for all of our bookkeeping needs. The spreadsheet, however, looks nothing like the original, though it is very effective for our business. At times I have doubted how long we will be able to continue to use it.

At 45 rental units we did try and switch over to professional bookkeeping software. What we quickly found was that it was slower than the system that we had in place. It was significantly more cumbersome, and it didn't track all of the things that we wanted tracked. To make matters worse, we were paying good money for something that didn't get the job done. Luckily, we had kept using our spreadsheet in tandem just in case there were any glitches in the new system. We switched back over to our spreadsheet after about six months with the professional software. I'm at the point where I believe that we can continue to use our system forever if we want to. It is easily expandable, so adding properties doesn't take very long. I suspect at some point when we hire office staff, we will need something that is more secure though. Right now neither of us worries too much, as only

Parham touches the spreadsheet, and she knows not to change any formulas, etc. I don't want to risk having office staff with the ability to adjust formulas and cells. If someone makes a change that goes unnoticed it could be a disaster trying to find the last backup without the change and then manually reentering everything from that point forward.

Once you have enough properties that you require a bookkeeping system, this will become yet another expense that you have that you didn't have when you started out. It is not a major expense, but again it is a cost that wasn't there with one or two rentals. When you add the cost of this system with the additional cost of hiring accountants, you will see that you need to offset these costs somewhere along the way. Failure to offset these costs will diminish your profitability and potentially your ability to continue to be competitive in the market.

Another major cost that will crop up is office space. Maybe you are lucky enough to have a spare room in your house that you can use as office space, maybe you are not. Either way, you are going to have to find some space that can be dedicated to work related activities. I like to think that we are in a paperless world and that wherever my computer is my office can be. That is a naive belief. You will need file cabinets, you will need a desk, you will need a printer and you will need a dedicated space. We have a physical file for each property that we own. In that file we keep copies of leases, material lists, warranty information, etc. We also have a separate file drawer just for the HUD-1 statements for our properties. Then there is the insurance and tax info, as well as a file on the utility bills for each property. Our desk is full, there is a drawer for printer paper, one for envelopes (you would be amazed at the amount of outgoing mail that we have), office supplies, etc. You may also want to treat your office like a work area. Hang motivational posters, pictures of your successes and reminders of your mistakes.

Our most important piece of wall furniture is a dry erase board with our to do list on it. It helps us keep track of each other's schedules and is a great communication board. Yes, we give each other lists of things to do, there is a lot to do and having it written down is a big help. Just like accounting and bookkeeping, your home office is yet another expense that adds up. Buying all of those items costs money, and finding a place for them costs space.

An even bigger expense that is in the same variety as the home office is storage space. We store massive amounts of stuff. "Stuff" is the technical term for necessities that may not be used all the time, but nonetheless need a home for the time being. An example of "stuff" is additional flooring from a project. Now we use the exact same flooring everywhere so we have less to store than before, but rest assured you are not going to throw away extra vinyl plank flooring. You will store it for the next project, or for later when repairs are required. Same goes with paint. Again, we now use only four colors/sheens of paint, but there was a time before we streamlined things. If you have 20 paint cans that is a lot of storage. Even with only using four colors of paint, we keep extra on hand of each one, and we have all sorts of paint products to store. We have oil-based primer, high hide oil-based primer, regular primer, ceiling paint, door paint, exterior paint, you get the drift. We store spare plywood, 3/4", 3/8" and 1/4". All of these things take up space, and this does not even begin to cover tools. I have every tool imaginable, from table saws to Sawzalls. In the end we require a storage facility to keep everything in.

Please do not think that you are going to solve this problem cost free by simply not giving your tenants access to the garage or shed on one of your properties. I have seen this done so many times. It almost always ends poorly, and even if it doesn't it still costs you the money that you intended to save in lost rent. If you have a garage on a property and don't include it in the rent, then you are shortchanging your company of the rent that it deserves for that property. You are also obligating yourself to go over to your tenant's house every time you need something. Either you or your tenant will get tired of this really fast. Tenants don't want you wandering around on their property whenever you want. It is disrespectful to them, and it will eventually result in headaches. Either they will give you work to do when you come over, or they will have something parked in the way of the shed.

It is important that you understand that as your business grows so does its needs, and you will start reducing your headaches in choosing to allocate cost to things that will help simplify your role in your business. All of these costs fall under the cost of doing business. You can do your best to minimize the costs of doing business by keeping your office and storage space to a minimum, adopting basic bookkeeping software, and you can even do things to minimize the costs of your accountant.

Understand that there are areas that you will find value in spending money on, and areas that you will not find value. I find value in having a good storage area, I am handy and work with my tools a lot. Perhaps you really thrive in an office setting, then make yourself a nice office and go easy on the storage. Just make sure that you understand these costs will come as your business expands and be prepared to meet them. I have seen many investors that have built their business up to this point and then sold, as they had failed to account for the cost of doing business. These landlords were running low margin businesses, that's code for landlords that consistently made bad purchases, and while they thought they were doing well, they actually weren't. They were not prepared for the inevitable. You should be prepared for the fact that as you grow, some costs will rise and margins will decrease.

Earlier I talked about ways to reduce costs. We did this in our business that year where we prioritized efficiency above growth. We continue to seek ways to offset these cost increases every day. The biggest way to offset the costs of growth is to use that growth to your advantage. As you start becoming a larger customer of your local providers, you should be able to obtain better pricing. You should start to get commercial accounts and agreements in place with significant reductions on retail pricing. One major area where we were able to take advantage of our growth was insurance. When we finally switched over to a commercial insurance policy, we realized immediate savings and that helped quite a bit with budgeting. Now that we are on a commercial policy, we pay monthly for our insurance. Previously we paid one year in advance on each policy and the payment was due on the month in which we had purchased the property. This meant that some months we made two or three insurance payments, other months we didn't make any. You can see where this made Parham crazy as she tried to manage the money all the while I was just out there with a buy, buy, buy mentality.

Chapter 25: Strategic Vision

Part of running a successful business for us has been the focus on having a balanced portfolio. We own numerous single-family homes, multi-family homes and a couple of small apartment buildings.

You will receive advice from many people along the way that sounds something like this: "buy single-family homes, they appreciate more" or, "buy single-family homes, they are easier to sell when the time comes" or, "buy apartments, you will grow your business faster" or, "buy duplexes, one unit will pay the mortgage and the other will be your profit". Take all of this advice, as none of it is bad. Eventually, you will have to make a choice in how you want your business to look. We listened to all of it and have developed a plan that I think lends itself better to long term business growth for *us*.

My goal is to be able to provide housing across the life cycle of a tenant. It is common knowledge that most people who rent will always rent, and I want to be there to provide housing for that tenant for life (provided that the tenant is a good tenant). With this in mind, we own one-bedroom apartments, one-bedroom houses, two-bedroom apartments, two-bedroom houses, three-bedroom houses, three-bedroom apartments, and four-bedroom houses. My ultimate goal is to be able to keep these good tenants renting from us as long as possible. We have had several tenants that have "upgraded" within our company. That is when they move from one of our smaller units to a bigger, more expensive unit. This is a win-win for everyone.

When tenants do decide to move on and buy their own homes we are there for that too, as we are licensed realtors. So even when a good tenant does leave, our strategy is to be able to assist them with that part of the process. This way we can even make money when they leave. We also position ourselves to get referrals from these tenants, which helps the realty side of the business.

To date we have had a limited amount of success with this integrated structure. I foresee quite a bit more success with this plan going forward. It is not for everyone or every business, but it works well for us and most importantly it works for our long term goals. You must decide what you want your business to be and how you see it growing. You may want your business to solely focus on single-family homes, as that is how most of us get started and that is perfectly fine. Or if you go another direction that is fine as well. Regardless of the direction you take, just make sure you are comfortable with it and that you stay focused.

As I was an engineer in a past life, I am fairly good at analyzing different things. One area that I have focused a lot on is profitability. Anyone who owns a business should look at this and look at it often. How profitable is my business? How profitable are my properties in area 1? How profitable are my properties in area 2? How profitable are my duplexes properties? How profitable are my apartments? How profitable are my single-family homes? These are several of the items that I look at. So first off, for ease of analysis, let's compare duplexes to single-family. We will keep the apartments out of the equation for right now. What I have found is that in my portfolio the cap rate on these is within two tenths of a percentage of each other. So, there is no real advantage for us to focus solely on one over the other.

Breaking it down a little more, let's look at operating areas. What I have found is that Area 1 is less profitable than Area 2 by a good margin. Focusing on Area 1 may not be that good of an idea. However, looking a little bit into the future, Area 1 has a much higher price ceiling than Area 2. Both these areas have very favorable margins, but one has little to no appreciation potential and lower operating margins. So why do I invest in Area 1 as well as Area 2? I do this as a way of hedging my bets and in acknowledgement of some things that are intangible. Area 1 isn't quite as profitable, but it is much, much easier to manage as the demographics lead to a better tenant base. The city that Area 1 is located in is also very well ran, which makes management easier as well. Easier equals less time and time is money, you can only have so many high intensity properties before you run out of time and have to hire full-time help. At the end of the day, everything comes down to your goals and your comfort level.

One last area that I have really started to look at with regards to profitability is the tenants themselves. I'm not looking at whether they look like slobs, the color of their skin, or what their ethnic background is, I am looking at their financial behaviors. Tenants that pay late are almost exclusively represented in our list of people who moved on while owing money.

Late fees do a lot to mitigate the total cost of money owed on the rent side. Our total late fees collected per year comes close to meeting the total amount of unpaid rents. This is a good offset, and really justifies the necessity of late fees. Late fees accomplish a couple of things: first, they help pay for the added office work associated with these tenants. Collecting late rent is extra work and can be a real pain. I don't work for free, especially when it comes to arduous work. Late fees also can be used to help encourage borderline tenants to move on.

The conversation usually goes something like this, "I know you don't want to pay the late fee, I can not waive it. We have waived it once already this year. You really ought to think about finding a place that is more affordable for you. We have some less expensive properties you could consider". (Conveniently, our less expensive properties are always occupied or in another area).

These are the tenants that usually move and don't pay the last month's rent on their way out. Worse things can happen. The security deposit will cover that loss. You just need to make sure that they move out without damaging the unit, as at that point all damages are not being covered by the deposit.

This is where I am really starting to look at costs, because that group of people who pay late coincidently is the same group of people that tend to leave places a mess when they move out. Looking at the additional cost to re-rent plus the cost of uncollected rents, I find that this group of people needs to be addressed sooner rather than later. This group represents the least profitable and most management intensive tenants you will have. It is enlightening to look at a pie chart of your business and see the categories that make up the largest amounts of your expenses. Those are the categories that need to be worked on. For us, those categories can be traced back to tenants with poor financial skills.

Chapter 26: Wrapping up

The single best part of our real estate success is not making lots of money or having great toys. If we only wanted those things the job in the mines was perfect, it provided a steady stream of income that could be used to buy whatever we wanted. In starting our business, we were after something that money cannot buy. Our purpose was, and still is, to have the ability to make a difference and be involved in our children's upbringing. Our lifestyle has not changed very much from when we first got married 13 years ago. The spending we do for ourselves is still about the same. We don't need the newest and best toys, and we don't spend a ton of money on gym memberships or fancy dinners. We do spend a good bit on our children, but not excessively. This kind of lifestyle is what enabled us to save money and afforded us the ability to invest in real estate. With our spending under control, we were able to find success. Now that we have found success and financial independence, we are able to truly make a difference.

I am able to be at all of our children's events, my wife is able to chaperone on field trips for our children's school and she volunteers quite a bit in the classroom. These are the types of things that really make all of the work that we put in worth it. We both volunteer as well. Being able to connect with our community and help out so much is very rewarding, and we wouldn't be able to do it without being financially independent. This is why it is so important to be successful, not so that you can buy toys, but so that you can make a difference in your community.

This is a simple business, but it's not an easy business. If you're looking for a "get rich quick" option, this is not for you. However, if you're looking for a way to guarantee long term wealth, real estate investing is a great option. More millionaires have been made in real estate than all other industries combined. With systems in place, the ability to financially assess deals and the right asset protection (insurance, lawyers, accountants, etc), there are very limited ways to lose. Growing a real estate business is methodical and the natural ebbs and flows in the economy will present opportunities through your business's growth cycle.

It's important to note that as you grow your business, your relationship with your W2 job will change. During this time, you'll start to get a sense that you don't *need* your W2 (at least you won't need it much longer) but you *want* it because for now it's an incredible tool that allows for and makes getting loans a lot easier. Just know this: W2's offer a very false sense of security. The system bates us with regular paychecks and health coverage (paired with a healthcare system that seems too complicated and expensive to navigate on our own). Take a moment and realize that your employer only "allows" you to work for them because the value you give them (your time and skillsets) exceeds the dollar amount they have to pay for you. The moment that this is no longer true, they'll kick you to the curb and not think twice about it. How secure is that really? Wouldn't you prefer being compensated in a way where there is equilibrium between the value you offer and the "payment" you receive? How about something you have better control over? As I spoke about earlier, health insurance is not difficult or expensive to get on your own. If I can do it with a family of five, so can you.

The key is to know your "why" and stay focused on your vision. You are completely capable and worthy of what you want in life, but you need to know clearly what that is and what you're doing it for. There will be times when things get tough, and your family and friends look at you like you're crazy for doing what you're doing. These are the times when calling on your WHY may be the only thing that pushes you forward. You have plenty of resources around you, get educated and surround yourself with high-achieving, experienced, reputable people who can help guide you. It's true, learning new skills and a whole new mindset as an adult is not easy. However, I'm sure you can agree that it may be possible. You need to start considering doing things in a way that feels outside of what you consider to be normal, in order to live a life that is anything but normal. I also urge you to stay humble and don't get frivolous with money when you start making some. This can be very tempting but once again, calling on your WHY will keep that in check.

Guys, we only live once. If even a small part of you is considering making the jump towards pursuing financial independence, there isn't a moment to waste. Get up, get out and get excited about this journey and don't look back.

About The Author

Zachary Weaver was born and raised in Chester, Virginia. Where he learned the value of hard work and accomplishment. Schooling was not where he excelled, he got himself through High School, and with the help of family, friends, & cash payments made it through college at Virginia Tech. Once in the real world Zach excelled as he found that leadership and people skills were far more important that technical skills. You can teach technical skills to employees, it is far harder to teach leadership. Zach credits his leadership skills to years and years of playing team sports as a child. "People don't realize the skills they are picking up playing a game of ball with the neighborhood kids."

Zach has a strong sense of right and wrong and can be difficult to work with if you end up on the side of "wrong". Luckily, for him he has a beautiful wife who is able to help moderate him and keep him focused on what really matters. You will rarely see Zach without Parham as the two of them make an inseparable team.

Zach's life revolves around Parham and the kids. Wyatt, Caroline, and Carson all play hockey and Zach spends more of his waking hours at hockey rinks than any other place, including his office. He's most proud of that!